S0-ADQ-073

Christiane Brandt Faris

"The Nicest Nazi"
CHILDHOOD MEMORIES OF WORLD WAR II

"The Nicest Nazi"
Childhood Memories of World War II
All translations by the Author

Copyright © 2014 Christiane Brandt Faris
All rights reserved.
Printed in the United States of America

ISBN 978-0-9886256-0-0

Published by

IONIC
PRESS

Cover and layout design, Margaret Ahrend Gaeddert

For Achim and Dottie,
Martin, Uta, Georg, and Jens.

ACKNOWLEDGMENTS

My gratitude goes to the many friends, students and colleagues who have asked and encouraged me to record my memories in writing. My compatriots Renate Wiggin, Barbara Farber, Christa Ritter, and the late Holocaust survivor Ora Harris and Lore Brandt have kept the old stories in perspective. I am indebted to many readers and conversation partners for their important suggestions and for the patient readings of my text: Ellen Berney, Margaret Flansburg, Mitzi McGuire, Sue Moss, Ann Dell, Joyce Stewart, Sandra Mayfield, Matt Randall, and Paul Young and Susan Seamans. Thanks also to my wonderful production team with Margaret Ahrend Gaeddert (no Umlaut) and my fabulous publisher Lolly Anderson. Most of all, I thank my family and my brother Achim in Germany, along with all the diligent hands who treasured and preserved old family letters and documents. I admire Achim's dedication to genealogy and his many publications which have been an inspiration to me in writing this memoir.

CONTENTS

CONTENTS

INTRODUCTION

"You are the nicest Nazi I have ever met."

This comment was shouted in my direction at a fund raising meeting of volunteers. A Nazi? I am a US citizen, but I was born in Berlin at the time of the Hitler Dictatorship, and I still hear long echoes from it.

The statement was meant as a funny compliment, perhaps a cute acknowledgment of my still audible foreign accent. But this was upsetting.

I know that my generation will never escape references to the Hitler period. And even my former American house invoked my German past. By coincidence I learned that a small upstairs room with a closet, a half bath, and a rickety external staircase was the residence of a Jewish couple who had escaped from that disastrous Hitler persecution in the 1930s. Their limited space in my house was a wide-open space of freedom. So far away in distance and time, this room is still a reminder of the darkest days of my country and history.

But at that meeting, the word Nazi was used in complete ignorance of the term's implications. Most regrettably, the term also has become popular in political parlance, whenever groups feel slighted by various authorities. Nazi does not identify me or my German countrymen; it refers to a particular historical movement of undeniable evil, viciousness, and mind control. The Enabling Laws, passed in Hitler's Third Reich solidified the government's power to punish anyone who was found neglecting his duties to the nation, in total disregard of existing democratic laws, thus creating a gangster regime.

The Nazi period went completely against the grain of what was good in the German culture. But sadly, compliance was the only way of survival.

Yet the question remains for me: did that period have an influence on my thinking, as a child, or even as an adult? How reliable are memories? While I can confidently state my opposition to the lawlessness and racial ideology of the Third Reich, a lingering uneasiness remains.

I was a child when every aspect of German life, back in the 1930s and '40s was imprinted by the orders and propaganda mandates of Hitler's Dictatorship (1933 – 1945) and by World War II (1939 - 1945).

My older brothers Arend and Achim experienced mandatory membership in the Hitler Youth and military service as teenagers. Yet we were only one generation removed from a time when the German Empire had included African and Chinese colonies and protectorates under Emperor Wilhelm II, from Kings and ruling aristocrats in Germany's complex history. Due to conditions after World War I (1914 – 1918), the Weimar Republic (1919 -1933) had failed as a state with a modern, democratic constitution.

With Hitler's election in 1933, the National Socialist German Workers Party (NSDAP) took control and would eventually erode any semblance of democratic process and justice. The ideological hunger for power and dominance of the Führer Adolf Hitler and his machinery of elite military groups (SS), rowdy Brown Shirts (SA), secret police agents (GESTAPO) and the threats of deportations and executions must be understood as separate from the very real experience of destruction that every German man, woman and child, and the populations of neighboring countries endured as consequences of the war.

Allied bombings and ground troops of the American, British, French and Russian Allied Forces brought the fanatical Reich to an end with an almost complete annihilation of major German cities, killing huge numbers of civilians. Although all members of the German military swore a mandatory oath of allegiance to the Führer, a clear distinction between the armed and the political forces was maintained.

More than Nazi doctrine, the Second World War molded my generation. Fear of bombings, destruction, deportation, food shortages, and loss became daily realities. In the post-war years, we school children went through a rather thorough process of re-education, of becoming acquainted with what was good, but had been suppressed, in our own culture, and we discovered the forms of democratic co-existence that the Western Allies brought.

We also learned about the atrocities of the Hitler regime, we saw newsprint of the Nuremberg War Crimes Trials, and we read the few available sources of the various Anti-Hitler movements. For us teenagers, those were years of discovery and endlessly heavy discussions about our past and our future. On a wider scale I wonder today: What was my history then? What is my history now?

The United States provided me with two scholarships for undergraduate and graduate study in Comparative Literature at American Universities. In the interim years, I finished my studies at Göttingen University in Germany and taught there.

I remained in the United States after my second academic year, married, and started a family and a teaching career. Without a doubt, my national background has had a profound influence on my perceptions of life and teaching. Now a retired professor of Modern Languages, I weigh my native language and culture in the knowledge of a controversial past.

The attempts to understand the events of the 20th century play an enormous part in Germany's self reflection. When older Germans speak of the War, they refer to the Second World War, which is still a presence today, after almost seventy years.

American students have a different understanding—there have been other military conflicts since World War II that were not fought on home territory but abroad: Korea, Vietnam, the Gulf War, Kosovo, the Iraq Wars, Afghanistan, and all the problems of the Middle East. My students or their families have been involved in some of these wars, making the German war a distant memory. Their parents may have been stationed at a German air base or have met German NATO military, and the recollections are positive and friendly.

Germans have developed a pacifist mentality. Officially still under Allied Agreement until German Unification, the military was not to be engaged in active fighting, but after the Fall of the Wall and with Unification in 1990, Germans have voted to participate in or reject current international wars.

Germans have contributed the largest contingent of historical immigrants to this country, and our two cultures are generally seen as quite closely related. Yet there are striking differences. The United States can claim an historical narrative based on one form of government, on revered founding documents, on one capitol city, one currency, one flag. By now Germany is the economic powerhouse of the European Union, and a country of picture book charm, but German history is marked by shifting forms of government, changed borders, changed capitol cities and identities, changed currencies, and changed flags.

For centuries, German literature and art have reflected a longing to understand the fragile human condition in harmonious and threatened conditions, with expressions of charmed life or bizarre distortions. While young Americans often have a positive outlook toward the future, Germans tend to be pessimistic.

When America thinks of the Jazz Age or the Golden Twenties, older Germans remember the worst ever unemployment and inflation, and current economic instabilities in the European Union recall the suffering of that long ago time. When the Depression struck the United States in the '30s, Germany was beginning to build Autobahns and recuperated in the early years of Hitler's technological modernity. The confident display of flags in the United States strikes Germans as peculiar, if not childishly patriotic. They have come to distrust their national flags and what they may represent.

These pages came together as a way of thinking about my own life. Memories from my childhood are strongly alive. But I am not writing an historical and objective report of the times, but a personal, sometimes emotional account.

To this day I am horrified by the facts, by what could have happened in my own life, and what I was spared. My central narrative focuses on our family life during the years after Germany's surrender, in 1945/46/47. But I can only do so by describing our experiences before the end of the war. In thinking back, I see the war years paradoxically as colorful adventures for a little girl. The post-war period, when I was a little more conscious of our environment, appears gray, a prolonged winter.

My family consisted of our parents, my two older brothers Arend and Achim and me, living in metropolitan Berlin, the German capital. Our grandparents in the northern German towns of Celle and Dissen played a hugely important role as well.

During the last years before armistice, we were scattered about and often did not know where the other family members were. Miraculously, we all found our way to my maternal grandmother's (Oma Auguste) house in the small, very historical city of Celle which had not been bombed.

We lived there under very limited circumstances. We had lost our home to bombs in Berlin, but we had survived. The members of my family and some homeless friends crowded together, scrambling to survive in the post-war confusion and lawlessness. There was scarcely any food and we had nothing to do. We had time in abundance, memories to sort out, and a senseless past to understand. On cold winter evenings we sat around the dining table, homebound by Allied curfew and lack of electricity, played games, talked, and read out loud.

The Brandt family vacationing at the Baltic Sea. (back to front) Mutti, Arend, Vati, Achim, Christiane; both brothers wear Hitler Youth shirts, 1941.

Classical literature and old family documents were read. Had it not been for the crowded conditions of the time, we would never have heard these family letters within the close family circle. We found that previous generations had similar fears and worries to ours.

In writing these pages, I am intrigued by the number and variety of letters and diaries that were preserved in our maternal and paternal grandparents' homes, even old letters from the United States. People wrote letters for many reasons—information, inquiry, or just to stay in touch. Today's many forms of communication displace the habit of personal writing, of deciphering someone else's signatures. These letters deserve safekeeping and are meaningful as reminders and memoirs. They speak of the writers' feelings and give us an insight today into joyous and hard times long gone. Some letters from my father are emotionally taxing to this day. The process of war-time recollection fascinates and astonishes me. Forgotten memories surface and weave themselves into patterns of coping with harsh realities.

My brother Arend, when alive, occasionally talked about the traumatic experiences that would later make living in Germany difficult for him. I am grateful for the many e-mail exchanges with my brother Achim on the subject. Both brothers shared the tragic plight of boys their age: state enforced separation from their families, constant fear of air raids, Hitler Youth *(HJ)* drills under the crude brutality of Nazi leaders, and frightening experiences in the military in their teenage years. These conditions traumatized their entire generation and left them with anxieties and claustrophobic attacks for the rest of their lives.

For me, there is some curious nostalgia about a life that seemed simpler in the midst of chaos and fear, but there is also recognition of ironies and incongruities that have become ludicrous, if not comical, over time.

I am not sure if any influences of that time had a hold on my life, other than leaving me with plenty of memories. I am not threatened by the Nazi label, but I am finely tuned to its implications.

I have discovered that the history of this "nicest Nazi I ever met" can only find expression in an effort of storytelling. All long-ago events will turn into stories. Some events defy rational understanding, some are heartbreaking, and some are comforting. I write to keep these memories alive and to share them.

Christmas 1939 in Berlin,
(left to right) Achim, Christiane,
Arend.

Our family represented the educated upper-middle class, living a comfortable, but not luxurious life. My brothers Arend and Achim were older than I was by 9 and 7 years respectively. They still took their little sister on subway rides from our suburb in the south of Berlin to the center of the city.

As an adult, Arend studied Archeology and History and became a teacher in Sweden, while Achim took a career in optical engineering. I studied German and English Literature at the University of Göttingen, and taught college for more than 30 years. A professor emerita now, I still live in the United States.

Our father was Dr. Wilhelm Brandt (Vati). He was very proud of his roots in Westphalia, in rural Dissen, where his ancestors had lived and prospered for many generations. A heart condition kept him from active service in World War I, but, having finished his law

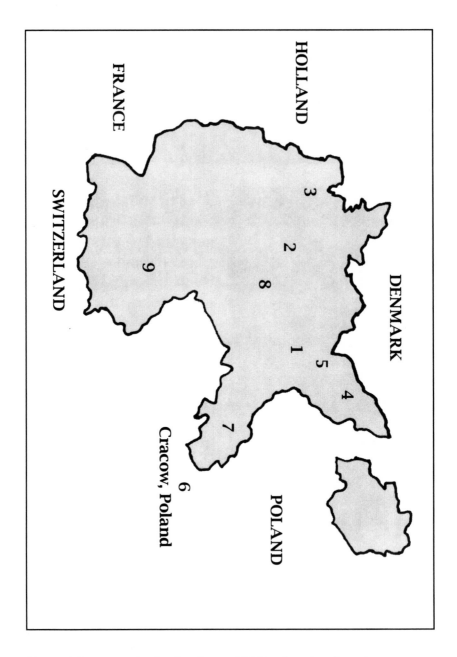

Map of Germany in the borders of 1918, showing locations mentioned in the text: 1) Berlin, 2) Celle/maternal grandparents, 3) Dissen/paternal grandparents, 4) Lauenburg on the Polish Corridor/our parents, 5) Stettin on the Baltic/Arend, 6) Cracow in Poland/Achim , 7) 8) evacuation from Berlin/Vati , 9) Nuremberg/ Philipp's trip to Dissen.

studies, he served as legal secretary and translator in a camp for French Prisoners of War. One of the Catholic dignitaries whom Vati took on a visitor's tour of the camp was the Papal Emissary to Germany, Nuncius Pacelli who would later become Pope Pius XII. Vati utilized his experiences from camp conditions in his dissertation on "The Rights of Prisoners of War." An internship on a large farming estate fostered his interest in land management and agricultural law.

In 1925, newly married, Vati found his first gainful employment in Lauenburg, in the far eastern province of Pomerania. This small town was on the border of formerly German lands which had become Polish (the Polish Corridor) under the international Peace Treaty after World War I. As a result, the German population had been expelled from the newly Polish areas. Homeless and impoverished refugees poured into the German border areas and needed to be resettled. There were overcrowded camps and food shortages. Vati's work with land reforms in the Weimar Republic (1919 -1933) tackled these conditions in hope of providing a better future for the traumatized population. A letter to his mother-in-law describes the demands of his work:

12. 21. 1924
The last few weeks and months were filled with work and stress for me. We (the Weimar Reich Government) bought several aristocratic estates and we are in discussions with owners for additional acquisitions. I am in charge of negotiating and securing finances for the newly established farmsteads on these lands. I also oversee the planning, construction and equipping of farms with operational inventories. Machinery, life stock, fruit trees, seed grain, fertilizer, tools

*and furniture need to be available. Beyond
that, the new farmsteads will grow into
communities and must be provided with
roads, water systems, schools and teachers,
firefighters, restaurants and beer bars, hospitals with maternity wards, and places of
worship, and it is all one big confusion all
the time. It is a colossal headache. One estate
near Lauenburg is in the planning stages for
being divided into 35 new farms, and I have
300 applicants. People have stormed my office and have followed me all the way home
to our apartment. But I like my work.*

A few years later, a promotion brought the young
family back into the central German area, where Vati
negotiated the purchase of private farmlands for the
construction of state-run Autobahns. During the Third
Reich, Vati worked on similar projects in Berlin, representing the interests of farming communities as well
as those of the state.

Appointed as legal counsel in the Reich Department of Agriculture, Food and Forestry, his work involved optimal use of the soil for adequate food production. For that reason, he was not drafted during
the war, and we grew up with a father in the house, a
rarity when men from all over the country were soldiers, away from their families. Vati was also appointed, but rarely called, as a specialty justice in the Third
Reich's Supreme Court.

Vati's task during the Third Reich and later was the
reorganization of aristocratic estates and lands that
had historically belonged to convents and monaster-
ies within the powerful, land owning Catholic Church.
Under Napoleon in the early 19th century, these lands
had been secularized and had become state property.
Modernization of these lands was an ongoing, urgent-

ly needed process. A thorough knowledge of the locations and conditions of these properties helped him escape from Russian captivity and survive at the end of World War II.

Essentially, Vati's work on land reform and water rights remained similar throughout his career: having studied these issues during the Empire of Kaiser Wilhelm, his work continued in the Weimar Republic, then as legal counsel in the Department of Agriculture in the Third Reich, followed by employment under the Marshall Plan during the Allied Occupation. And finally, as legal expert for the State of Lower Saxony and the Federal Republic of Germany (West, established in 1949), and for the burgeoning Common Market at the inception of today's European Community. For his work, he received the German Marshall Plan medal, and, upon retirement, the Order of Merit, first class, from the President of the Federal Republic of Germany.

Like many members of our generation, my brothers and I often discussed our father's involvement with Nazi ideology. Not even having a choice, he had joined the party early. By a law of 8.20.1934, all civil servants and military personnel had to swear allegiance to the Fuehrer of the German Reich, Adolf Hitler: to obey and fulfill all duties accordingly. My father did so as well. His expertise fit right into Nazi thinking.

The Nazi Party idealized the concept of *Blut und Boden* (blood and soil), of anything organically brought forth from the holy womb of Mother Earth. Conquering more land in the East for the "superior" German folks was their justification for war. Labor camps, concentration camps, and military installations all cut into arable lands.

How much did he know about the Holocaust atrocities? Had he unknowingly contributed? Was he one of the millions of silent enablers? Was he the good civil servant with or without personal integrity? Rather, he may have thought that he served the country, not the ruling party. He must have felt trapped in the contradictions between an objective law and the totalitarian abuses by the National Socialists.

These problems caused moral and ethical conflicts for many Germans. Vati's work ensured that farming and the production of food stuffs could continue. After the collapse of the regime in 1945, all German males with previous state employment underwent Denazification hearings by the Allies.

Vati was arrested, then let go and placed in the middle category, class 3 out of 5. Our attempts at identifying legal texts from his pen have not been successful. It was too long ago! There was no evidence of personal support for the system, and he did not indoctrinate his children. Letters found after his death and written in code speak of his contempt for the Nazis.

Calendar image showing Mutti Edith Hebbeler as a student of weaving at the Arts-and-Crafts School in Dresden, 1923.

Our mother (Edith Hebbeler Brandt) died of pneumonia when I was barely three years old. She had trained as a weaver in an Arts-and-Crafts school in Dresden. Memories of her were most likely kept alive in stories. I do not remember any feelings of loss, but my brothers, at age 10 and 12 remembered the emptiness of never seeing her again. Nevertheless, boys at that time were expected to overcome personal feelings of sadness with manly courage.

Gertrud Hebbeler, Celle, 1910.

Our mother's sister Gertrud ("Trude") Hebbeler, recently divorced, came to take care of us children and their father. She thought of this engagement as a short interlude only, intending to return to her position in the publishing industry. Gertrud had always known what she wanted. Several photos depict Gertrud, the middle daughter, as an adventurous child: in a lace dress on a bicycle, playing tennis, or in a row boat, shockingly exposing her bare arms. Her father Karl Hebbeler had picked this daughter as a substitute son to cultivate and promote his own intellectual interests. Besides her domestic training, and after the common nine years of public school for girls, Gertrud received private tutoring in Mathematics and Latin, in Literature and History and Art Appreciation.

But with the general patriotic enthusiasm for World War I, Gertrud discovered her social-mindedness and became a nurse. She worked in a makeshift field hospital that she had known from the days when it was a garden restaurant and dance hall. Training and clinical work as a mid-wife followed.

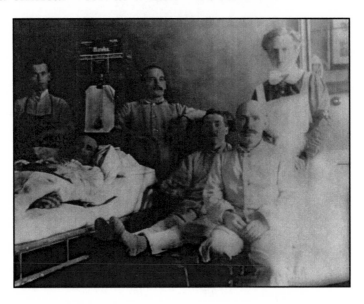

Nurse Gertrud Hebbeler in a World War I field hospital, 1915.

And then Gertrud folded up her nurse's uniform and enrolled in Library School at the University of Cologne. As a student, she traveled on her own in England and Italy. For years, Gertrud worked for the Harrassowitz Company in Leipzig as editor of *Jahrbuch der Bücherpreise*, an annual catalog listing sales prices for rare books in international auctions.

When she came to live with us in 1939, we motherless children called Gertrud "Mutti" right away, although she was our aunt. As propriety would have it, she slept in my room; perhaps one of the reasons why we became so very close. Vati and Trude married four years later. She was a loving and beloved stepmother, and never returned to her original profession.

Publication by Gertrud Hebbeler.

Vati's parents Franz and Clara Brandt lived right above the country store they owned in Dissen. Franz sold the store when he retired. The early contact with a small town's country population influenced our father in deciding on his future career. Opa Franz was no longer alive when we visited.

Coming from the hectic and increasingly dangerous life in metropolitan Berlin, the whole family often spent relaxing vacations in the large old house and garden. The house had no running water: there was a huge pump with a polished brass lever in the kitchen, and the bathroom's toilet shot all waste right down to a holding tank.

Oma Clara and Opa Franz Brandt in Dissen.

The Brandt family vacationing in Dissen from Berlin, 1942: (left to right) Oma Clara, Vati, Arend, Achim, Mutti Trude, Christiane.

Vati loved to hike with us children in the mountains of the nearby *Teutoburger Wald* (Teutonic Forest) which he knew from his childhood. He was a steady, brisk walker, always telling us that slow strolling would make us tired. With sandwiches in our rucksacks, we marched for hours before we reached the right picnic spot where sweet, wild strawberries and raspberries grew. Vati shortened the long walks by telling stories of the region. The dusty country road to the foot hills, lined with apple trees had always been a military road, since ancient times, he said. A small creek had once been the borderline between two kingdoms.

When I stood on that bridge, I could have one foot in each kingdom, and I imagined soldiers pulling me in both directions until POP! I ripped apart. It was like tales from the Brothers Grimm come alive. We listened to his reports of the defeat of a whole Roman Army by the cunning chieftain Herman the German, some two thousand years ago, and that might have happened right there under our feet.

We climbed the highest elevation in the mountains, the *Hankenüll*, and Vati explained that in the Westphalian dialect of the area the *Hankens* were dwarves and gnomes, and this was where they lived. I would forever search for the *Hankens* under mossy tree roots and near creeks.

Franz and Clara Brandt had four sons. My father was the oldest. His brother Otto succumbed to lung injuries from World War I, his brother Hermann was killed by German bombs when stationed with the occupying German force in Holland in World War II,

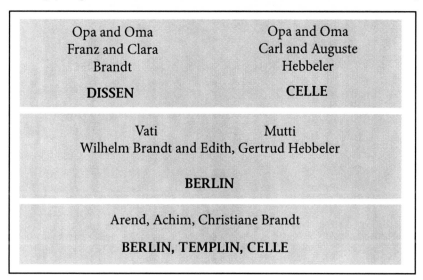

Opa and Oma Franz and Clara Brandt **DISSEN**	Opa and Oma Carl and Auguste Hebbeler **CELLE**

Vati   Mutti
Wilhelm Brandt and Edith, Gertrud Hebbeler

BERLIN

Arend, Achim, Christiane Brandt

BERLIN, TEMPLIN, CELLE

Our families in Dissen, Celle, Berlin.

and a baby brother had died as an infant. In 1939, our grandmother Clara Brandt received a deed of conferral for the *Ehrenkreuz der Deutschen Mutter* (Cross of Honor of German Motherhood), third class, from the Third Reich. A facsimile signature of Adolf Hitler identifies the document as an example of Nazi ideology, meant to increase the country's birth rates. Such a certificate would encourage women to have more children, it was thought. The third class honor was given to mothers of racial and medical purity with at least four children. At the time of conferral, two of Oma Clara's four sons were no longer alive.

Cross of Honor of German Motherhood
for Clara Brandt, signed by Adolf Hitler.

Mutti's parents Karl and Auguste Hebbeler (Opa Karl & Oma Auguste) lived in the very historical city of Celle, in the northern flatlands. Karl had studied Chemistry in Leipzig. As an enterprising young man, he went to London, where Queen Victoria's German consort had created a friendly climate for his countrymen, and where the purchase of a pharmacy was less restricted than in Hamburg.

The two older Hebbeler daughters, Annie and Gertrud, were born in England, which would later present difficulties for them in Nazi Germany, as they were suspected of being enemy spies. Oma Auguste learned to speak English and could tell us stories about all the mistakes she had made in the foreign language.

Grandfather (Opa) Karl Hebbeler in front of his pharmacy Deutsche Apotheke in London, 1895.

The invention of a portable filtering system for drinking water would eventually bring Karl and his family back to Germany, to a location near the mineral mines necessary for his filters, and that was Celle. Karl built a large house and a splendid terraced garden for his wife and three daughters Annie, Gertrud, and Edith.

Karl's inventions for the Berkefeld Filter Company proved to be much in demand in the colonies of England, France and Germany, and on the battlefields of World War I. The many picture postcards still around documented his travels all over Europe to introduce the filter system at medical conventions. When we visited, the filtering system was no longer in use, but Opa Karl's beautiful ceramic filter

The Hebbeler family in Celle, 1903, (left to right) Oma Auguste, Opa Karl, daughters Edith, Annie, Gertrud.

vessels were still around and served for storage in the house and garden.

Oma Auguste was the daughter of a learned and strict Lutheran supervisor of churches and schools on the Atlantic coast near the Danish border in Germany's North. She would talk about her memories of sea captains, pirates, Danish skirmishes, of hurricanes and shipwrecks and flotsam.

When the family visited Celle from Berlin, Oma Auguste had been widowed for some time. Her large

The author discovered an antique Berkefeld
Filter container in a restaurant in Singapore,
a former British colony, 2000.

house had been subdivided into apartments with her rooms on the first floor. I loved to sleep in the bed that had been Mutti's, a long time ago. Its white enameled latticework with gold knobs and twisting vines invited sweet dreams. There were old toys and books from the previous generation and from Aunt Annie's children. These cousins were older and we rarely saw them. A favorite entertainment was Oma's trunk full of dress-up clothes: a circus performer's glittering dress, clown outfits, funny hats, parasols, and long floating dresses from Oma's youth.

The von Schluters lived on the second floor. An elderly woman teacher occupied the third floor. There was ample attic space, a fruit cellar, a separate cellar for the furnace and coal storage, a sandy yard by the former coach house with more attic space and old stables to explore. Mrs. Kohlmeier and her sons Werner and Theo, my age, lived in the converted coach/ washhouse, while Herr Kohlmeier was a soldier in Russia.

I was curious and a little scared to visit the von Schluters. A mysterious aura of quiet calm hung in their sitting room. The old gentleman still had the bearings of a Prussian cavalry officer. In his glory days, some thirty years prior, he had been a high-ranking forester in Kaiser Wilhelm's vast eastern woods. He had also been a personal currier, entrusted with important mail between St. Petersburg and Berlin—between Czar Nicholas and his cousin Emperor Wilhelm.

Achim in garb from Oma's dress-up trunk, the 3 Brandt children in Celle, summer 1941.

The walls in the von Schluter apartment were festooned with trophies of his former career: moose heads and wild boars stared at me with glass eyes in the dim light, and massive antlers, horns and tusks poked out between the heads. The sofa and chairs were covered with various forms of animal skin. When I ran my fingers along the furry chair legs, I could feel the direction of the beast's hair growth. The dining table rested on huge elk legs with hooves. Frau von Schluter served tea cakes on plates with roaring stags. It was intriguing to imagine that long ago Mutti and her sisters, wearing white lace dresses, had played in this room that now looked like a hunting lodge.

LIFE IN BERLIN:
MOVING AWAY 1943

The apartment in the southern district of Lankwitz was comfortable and sunny, with a loggia overlooking a park, and a balcony by the bedroom. There was no elevator; we walked up in a wide stairwell to our apartment on the third floor. A physician, Dr. Wentzel, lived and practiced at the other end of our landing. All apartments had central heating and warm water in the kitchen and bathroom, for which coal supplies were stored in the cellars. There was a small gas stove in the kitchen. We all knew how to scrub ourselves clean with soap, a washrag and warm water in the bathroom's small sink. We had an occasional bath in the tub, but showering was uncommon.

Our live-in maid Gretel did the cleaning and cooking. Food was sufficiently available, although strictly rationed per week and by weight: meat, fats, dairy products, bread, fruit, sugar. The convenience of today's shopping mall or grocery store did not exist. Housewives would stand in line, waiting with their shopping bags at the butcher shop, at the greengrocer's, the baker's, at the dairy store, and at the general store for sugar, coffee, flour and soap. Not that there were large quantities of each item, but they all needed to be carried home and hauled upstairs. Food could only be obtained with officially issued ration cards.

Occasionally the family gathered on weekend afternoons to play games. One Saturday, Oma sent a package with gingerbread and a board game from the local Celle cookie factory.

Eat your fill
of Cookies from
Trill

Celle Cookie
Factory

The goal of the game was to advance through the Trill warehouse, through the kitchens for dough making and baking, on to the glazing tables, to the wrapping stations, and finally to the garage and on to a delivery truck. On the game board, the Trill warehouse offered a fantastic supply of baking ingredients, such as we had never seen with our meager ration cards. There were barrels full of butter, sacks of raisins, vats of honey, boxes of sparkling sugar crystals, exotic spices, and chocolate chips. Mouthwatering! I loved looking at this wonderland, but I detested playing. Achim always won while I got kicked out and sent back to start over! I would whine and cry and hit him under the table.

All articles of clothing were rationed as well, with allotments of socks, underwear, shoes, coats, and all else, detailed on ration cards per age group, sex, and allowed time period. These ration cards were presented for every purchase, and the seller snipped off the appropriate coupon square.

As a result, I grew up in anything usable from the boys and the adults that had been passed down to me. Most of all, I hated my brothers' cast-off one piece undergarments, which had a slit in the wrong place for a little girl in the bathroom. I felt encased in thick cotton from my neck to my knees. A simple pee required to unhook the three buttons on a flap in the back, pull the fabric in the right position, sit down on the toilet, and then re-hook the whole panzer.

My dresses were made of reused and restyled skirts from Mutti or Oma, or from duvet covers and bed linens that had worn thin. Shoes were another problem. If outgrown, the tips were cut off, leaving toes to stick out and grow longer. After the death of Oma Clara in Dissen, I became the proud owner of her buckled, high heeled house shoes. Made of warm felt and meant for indoor wear, these fashion items took me to school through snow and ice, as if walking on stilts. Nothing was ever wasted; recycling was a way of life, sometimes fostering creative solutions.

Television had not been invented yet.

Ration coupons for eggs, potatoes, bed feathers, and textile coupons with specific items allotted by date.

The boys set up their electric trains, I had my dolls and a doll house, Vati read, Mutti had mending or needle work. The only telephone and the one radio set were placed on Vati's desk in the living room.

Radios were a relatively new invention; they were

mass produced and available in two sizes at low cost. These *Volksempfänger* (peoples' receivers) were preset to NSDAP (*National Sozialistische Deutsche Arbeiter Partei*, National Socialist German Workers Party) propaganda stations. Listening to foreign stations, particularly the BBC, could result in the most severe punishment, even execution.

On Sundays, we went to Berlin's impressive museums, to the Zoo, or to the Botanical Gardens. We visited a special friend at the Aquarium: a rare albino eel that had been caught by fisherman Nolke whose fishing and boat shop was just across the Aller River from Oma's house in Celle. Trips to Potsdam were fun. We visited Frederic the Great's 18th century palace Sanssouci, where all visitors scooted around in floppy felt slippers in order to protect the inlaid floors.

Vati and Mutti did not take us to party rallies or parades. Like every German adult, they had to be members of the NSDAP and other organizations that cast a network of enforced membership on the civil population. I still have a letter reminding Mutti that she had not paid her fees to the National Socialist Association for German Writers. I do not recall any enthusiastic support for the party or its racial ideology. Mutti's sentiment is clearly expressed in a letter of 1939, at the beginning of the war:

The medical conditions are catastrophic in Berlin. The many Jewish physicians who can no longer practice are sorely missed. The remaining doctors are overworked, and it is flu season.

The letter was written shortly after the atrocities of *Kristallnacht* had been committed in November 1938 against the Jewish population and their businesses in all major cities. As is obvious from this letter, Mutti had become aware and regretted the sanctions imposed on Jewish professionals. Vati, too, would express his disdain for the Third Reich in carefully coded letters to Mutti.

Three unusual events in our apartment stand out in my retrospective memory:

- A Hitler Youth boy *(HJ)* showed up at the door and collected Mutti' skiing gear. Even as a little girl I could tell that this sacrifice was hard for her. She had lived in Munich before, and loved the sport in the Bavarian Alps. The collection effort was ordered in support of the Russian Offensive, in 1941 or '42. Hitler expected a quick victory in the East, completely miscalculating the vast distances and furious temperatures of the country. The troops had been sent out for a short fighting season in the summer. With a near total lack of equipment and clothing, the German men were overpowered and massacred in the harsh Russian winter.

- I also remember Dr. Wentzel's maid in the doorway to their apartment. She was crying and yelling in anguish through the stair well. She had just received notice of her brother's heroic death as a soldier for the German fatherland in Russia.

- And then a fabulous present arrived one day at our door, like unexpected heavenly manna. It was a wicker basket, almost as tall as I was. At eye level I could see that the surprise gift was filled to the rim with schnitzel meat, a ham, sausages, several bottles of wine, coffee, bread, butter, jams, a whole round of cheese, pretzels, a cake, apples, fresh carrots, honey, and on the top lay a fluffy, freshly hunted rabbit. This was a bribe for Vati, and he sent it right back.

When Arend and Achim took me on subway rides into the city, I was thrilled to find large posters on the trains and in the stations. Not knowing that these were propaganda tools, I particularly loved *Kohlenklau*, the coal filcher, a grinning, unshaven little guy who winked at me while he was stealing coal and other resources. *Kohlenklau* was married to *Wasserplansch* (Water Squish). She was fat and sloppy and did she ever waste water! Cheerful little rhymes explained

Kohlenklau, one of many anti-waste posters

that these two sniffed around our houses, eager to snatch heat, water, and electricity, even other things. We should never allow these thieves to steal from us! All these resources were needed for our armament industry.

And then there were scary placards of *Feind Hört Mit,* (the enemy listens in) which warned that dissenters might spy on the Reich and one needed to toe the party line. The fact that I remember these posters speaks to the success of this propaganda campaign.

It was mandatory for all boys from the age of ten to join the *Jungvolk* (the young folks, the lowest level of the Hitler Youth, *HJ*). I remember seeing Arend and Achim in their uniforms of beige shirts with bolos of knotted leather, black corduroy knee pants, the *HJ* emblem on their belt buckles, and knit stockings. We would stand by the entrance to the subway station, where heavy pedestrian traffic was expected. Achim would yell: "Give to the *Winterhilfswerk*" as he rattled the sealed, domed tin can. I held a box of trinkets that donors could select from for the Winter Aid Program. It seemed that different cheerful little items were supplied every week. There were colorful glazed heads glued to pins, jigsaw figures, embroidered butterflies. We had a large collection of these heads at home, and I doubt that we had purchased them. They were familiar fairy tale characters: Hänsel and Gretel, a grandmother, a witch, a policeman, a crocodile, Cinderella, Little Red Riding Hood and the wolf. We stuck those heads on matchsticks and used them as puppets for long make-believe conversations.

Vati had to sell Winter Aid trinkets also. His pockets rattled with small Hohner harmonicas in lacquered red wood shells with embossed nickel sides. They played a few tones and could be worn on a string around the neck. But how many harmonica necklaces did one need?

The Third Reich had inherited deplorable economic conditions from World War I and the Weimar Republic. In an effort to alleviate hunger, the Winter Aid Program was developed to elicit public donations for the winter seasons. When the program turned out to be successful, it was expanded to year long obligatory participation, with the income used for various party endeavors.

It was hoped that people would want to collect whole sets of the small trinkets, which were made by folk artists and unemployed craftsmen. Contributions were automatically deducted from paychecks, and even those too poor to pay taxes had to pay their monthly fees.

A similar effort of enforced public charity was the *Eintopfsonntag* (one pot Sunday), mandating that families eat a Sunday meal of thin soup that cost no more than 50 pennies. Uniformed Brown Shirts might knock at the door and collect the differences in cost to a regular meal.

It was required that *HJ* uniforms be worn for all special events and assignments. Arend and Achim complained that the icy winter winds of Berlin left them with frozen, blue knees in their short pants, which did not make them into strong future soldiers, as the party propaganda claimed. In the privacy of our apartment, the boys sometimes stood at attention and recited a dutifully memorized Hitler speech in the clipped voice of a Hitler Youth leader: "*der deutsche Junge*" (The German boy of the future must be slender and supple, swift as greyhounds, tough as leather, and hard as Krupp steel).

The *Jungvolk* and Hitler Youth organizations created a system of ranks and obligations, for which special terms had to be used. My brothers called each other and their friends by the official, age appropriate title: "*Pimpf* Brandt, *Pimpf* Schneider, *Pimpf* Meier." Arend as the older one had gained the designation of *Fähnlein-führer* (small flag leader), with the flag being a group of boys. In this role, Arend spent many evenings in endurance training or mandatory marching exercises until late into the night.

The issue of uniforms took on a personal meaning

when Arend was about to be confirmed in the Lutheran church. Confirmation was an act of defiance in itself and uniforms were required. Mutti made sure that Arend wore his regular clothes.

As a first grader, I was too young to have been a uniformed member of *BdM,* the league of German girls. I walked to our neighborhood elementary school in Berlin. Not much effort was devoted to learning, as instructions about our patriotic duties to the fatherland took up most of our time. We were also instructed on behavior in case of air raids during the day: run home as fast as possible at the sound of the pre-warning siren; stay in the school shelter when a sudden full alarm sounds.

Of greatest importance was our effort at trash collecting. As I remember, *Altmaterial* included string, paper, the foil lining from cigarette boxes, fabric scraps, bones, hair, and stamps. We learned that foil papers were useful to disrupt the enemy's radar systems, and the hair from our mothers' and neighbors' combs was woven into warm uniform cloth for our brave soldiers. Bones were good for fertilizer and soap making. After all, cleanliness was a prevalent virtue in the Reich.

The school gym had been converted into a dimly lit warehouse, and we children lined up every morning to get our contributions evaluated and recorded on grade cards. It was my turn. Barehanded the teacher reached into my envelope and pulled out Mutti's loose hair.

"One point for hair. No bones? Next in line."

Meat was severely rationed, and bones were hard to come by. I once collected a few meager soup bones from the neighbors, but on the way to school hungry dogs attacked me and I tossed my bone treasure to them, naively thinking that I would find it after school on the way home. But no such luck! At another time, a heavy rain soaked through my paper sack with fabric scraps. I picked up the wet rags and gathered them in my short skirt and walked on, embarrassed, exposing my underpants. Achim recalls an outing during school time to collect flowering weeds for herbal teas.

We received movie tickets as rewards for our trash collecting. I remember sitting in an afternoon showing of *Dick und Doof* (Fat and Stupid) when the sirens sounded and all the children ran to their homes. This comic duo was actually the German version of Laurel and Hardy. Surprisingly, the cinema was still running such a program, although Hitler had ordered all imports of foreign films be stopped.

Civilian men still in the city were called for war-related services. Vati's immediate supervisor was a devoted Nazi. He was the rat catcher of the neighborhood and would come to the apartment to question Vati on his diligence, all swelled up with the importance that the party uniform had given him.

As air raid warden for the block, Vati now checked daily on every apartment's black-out installations, making sure that only dim light bulbs were turned on while heavy blankets covered the windows completely. In the absence of street lamps, light reflecting signs were painted on house fronts to direct pedestrians in the pitch dark city to underground shelters.

It was thought that British night bombers would easily lose their target orientation when cities were invisible from above in complete black-outs. Vati checked shelter readiness in each apartment's cellar: again, low lights, chairs along the walls for the residents, a clean bucket for "bath room breaks," pick axes near emergency exits which were needed to break through walls into neighboring cellars. Vati's duty also included attic inspections to count sand sacks and water buckets in case a fire was to be extinguished. In view of the severity of the bombings, these provisions appear ludicrous today.

We were all used to nightly air raids. After the United States had entered the war in 1941, raids increased gradually, with the American Air Force flying during the day, and the Royal British Air Force flying in at night. Planes had been developed with the capacity to carry fuel and bombing loads to the inland location of Berlin, and return safely back to their bases. Howling sounds of warning sirens roused us from sleep; we got up and tried to dress fast and in confusion.

Mutti complained about my lack of cooperation as I slipped back into bed and pulled my socks and pants off. But it was not safe to stay above ground during air attacks. We grabbed our packed rucksacks and gas masks and stumbled into the converted cellar room in complete darkness. Arrows in night-glow paint along the black stair well showed us the way. We children wore glow pins, which we charged in sun light: flowers, animals, fish, and hearts.

There were several children in our shelter. We stayed in bunk beds and yelled at the outside noise to disguise our fear. One night of raids was really frightening. We listened to the whistling hiss of approaching bombs, followed by massive detonations.

"Listen to that racket! Bam! Those bandits are throwing everything they have at us! Pots and pans! Wish I could do that! There went a skillet! A bathtub! Bricks!"

If an air raid lasted till after midnight, school did not start until ten o'clock the next morning, and we always hoped for a late "all clear" siren. Back upstairs in the apartment, we found that windows had blown open from air pressure following the explosions, and our canary bird Piepsi had flown away—or at least that was what I was told.

The glass in the dining room door looked like a spider's web, cracked and splintered into thousands of pieces, but still beautifully suspended in the frame. Repairs were made, and made again. Our building was not hit that night, but we could tell that great damage had been done close by.

Arend and Achim were already in secondary school, which was not in the neighborhood. Riding the subway to and from school became dangerous as surprise raids and alarms could sound off during the day, and the boys would have to hunt for shelter away from home.

Vati and Mutti decided in early 1942 to place my two brothers in a boarding school outside of Berlin, in Templin, where intellectual culture was still valued. I had been a single child one summer before, when Arend was drafted for *Wehrertüchtigungslager*, a camp for pre-military instruction, and Achim participated in mandatory *Kinderlandverschickung*, a program that sent city children to the countryside.

From their comments it was obvious that they did not like the enforced summers away from home. Both programs were promoted as fun vacation camps, but the hidden intention was the removal of children from family influence in favor of integrating them into the *Volk* (folks, people). The *Volksgemeinschaft* idealized belonging to the clan of like minded, racially pure Aryan people and eradicating anyone in violation of the race purity laws. This concept of a superior community where humans mingled with powerful Gods and battle-ready men, such as Wodan, Thor, the Valkyries and the beloved hero Siegfried exploited the stories of Northern Germanic mythology.

The term *Volk* gained currency in every-day language, such as *Jungvolk, Volksaufkärung* (propaganda), *Volksmund* (oral tradition), *Volksschule, Volksempfäenger* radio, *Vöelkischer* Beobachter (a newspaper), *Volkswagen, Volkssturm (peoples storm troopers, old men and young boys).* Political indoctrination into the *Volksgemeinschaft* included harsh physical training and was directed by rough party bullies. For Arend and Achim, the closeness of our family proved a stronger power than the elusive membership in an anonymous Nordic *Volk.*

Moving to a boarding school was a serious decision for all, but the boys would be in a safe environment, they would be together, and they would make new friends. For me, it was a more permanent good-by, as I would only see my brothers occasionally at vacation times.

Templin had been a historical institution for the education of sons of the Prussian nobility, but commoners were accepted. I became familiar with the names of my brothers' new aristocratic friends. Prussian virtues like honorable service to the country, a sense of duty, study and learning, hard work, self reliance, frugality, ethical responsibilities, and a stout Lutheran faith were at the basis of Templin's curriculum. It is not surprising that these values were in conflict with Nazi ideology and would lead young members of Prussian aristocratic families to active involvement in anti-Hitler Resistance groups.

Due to the academic rigors of Templin, Achim experienced the school as a harsh environment. He was 12 years old, had lost his mother, missed his family and would soon be parted from his brother who was to be drafted into teenage military service.

Increased bombings made living in Berlin more and more chaotic. I remember sharing our bedroom with neighbors whose apartment had been destroyed, and the mother of my neighborhood friend Axel had suffocated under a collapsed building. There was rubble in the streets, and we were warned that unexploded bombs might be hidden under the debris. The air was grey with dust and cement particles that settled

This classic children's book The Bunny School
survived the fire storms of Berlin.

on our lips and teeth. A "splinter trench" was dug into the park along our apartment block as a temporary shelter in case a secure bunker could not be reached in time.

After the boys had left, Vati decided that Mutti and I should leave Berlin as well and move to the relative security of Oma Auguste's house in Celle. In preparation for our move to Celle, Mutti packed our suitcases with items we needed and wanted to take along, including a few toys and favorite books, some of which I still have.

Mutti left two more cases with documents, photos, silver, and other things for a later move. Vati remained behind, attending to his work, which became more and more disrupted. We took the train to Celle and included a short vacation trip to visit Oma Clara in Dissen. While in Dissen, we heard about the devastating firebombing of Hamburg on the radio.

A bombing survey in the United States recorded that the atomic bomb on Nagasaki did not cause as much damage as did the 9,000 tons of explosives dropped on Hamburg by the British and American Air Forces combined. With a large port, shipyards and U Boat pens, oil refineries and Alfred Nobel's Dynamite factory nearby, Hamburg was a vital industrial center. While the city had been bombed from the beginning of the air strikes, and would continue to be under attack until the virtual end of the war, "Operation Gomorrah" devastated the city beyond recognition in eight deadly days in July 1943.

Fuel from damaged ships spilled into the Elbe River and the many city canals and ignited. While the population sat in shelters below, blockbuster bombs burned the city in superheated fires that sucked oxygen from the air and caused death by suffocation. Forty thousand fatalities and as many injuries were recorded.

Surviving women and children were evacuated, and the city remained off limits for the duration of the war. British General Harris' intention of forcing Hitler to surrender by total demoralization and destruction of the civilian populations is still controversial, and did not achieve its goal as the war continued for almost another two years.

Hamburg was just north of Celle. For a few days, while we were in Dissen, Oma Auguste made room in her house for an evacuated family from the burning city, until they could find refuge with relatives elsewhere. That a stranger had slept in my white dream bed made me very uneasy. It was an intrusion into my privacy, perhaps a first realization that war was everywhere, that people became homeless nomads, that personal belongings could be lost forever, that privacy had become meaningless, and that strangers helped each other.

We would shortly lose all belongings in our apart-

Refugee Pass for Christiane Brandt.

ment in Berlin as well, but we had a home with Oma. I still have my refugee pass as a reminder.

Train travel was no safer than staying at home. Owing to unexpected air raids, trains no longer ran on schedule; they often did not run at all, or were late, always being overcrowded. Transfers to other lines could take hours of waiting on cold and drafty platforms. Travelers with heavy suitcases pushed their way through the waiting crowds. Getting onto a train was most important. People shoved their luggage of boxes and rucksacks through the train windows or climbed in that way; standing closely packed in the compartments during the trip or sitting on suitcases was the norm. I was told to scream if I saw men exposing themselves or felt them fingering me.

I never experienced a direct train hit, but plenty of stories circulated about such hits when travelers sought refuge under the heavy train chassis. I do remember a traumatic evening in the train station of Bielefeld, where our route transferred to the Dissen train.

The city had been bombed that day. Our train pulled into the station and all passengers fled into the underground tunnels that connected the various platforms. Children screamed as adults were searching for family members in the dimly lit and overcrowded tunnels. The air was grey and heavy from smoke. It was very frightening.

When the connecting train finally pulled out at night, we saw burning buildings close to the station. When we traveled during the day, we could clearly see damaged buildings with whole walls sheared off, or the iron structures of stairs and balconies hanging in mid air, or windowless walls reaching like skeleton fingers into the sky. Chimneys often withstood the bombings, but they were purposeless with no stoves or furnaces connected. Even for years after the war, one could see light-reflecting arrows pointing to useless air raid shelters.

A CITY AND HOUSE TO EXPLORE
IN CELLE, SUMMER 1943

Oma had lived in Celle for almost fifty years. Located in the northern low lands, Celle lies some 100 miles south of Hamburg, about 30 miles north of Hanover, and the sleepy town of Bergen-Belsen is even closer. The surrounding landscape is not spectacular, but rather displays a melancholy, harsh beauty, desolate in parts.

Landscape near Celle.

Millions of years ago, the ice age had washed in impoverished white sands that grow only woodsy heather plants. In the summer, the area erupts into blankets of pink heather blooms, set against dark, low juniper shrubs. Beekeepers produce a delicious honey from heather blossoms in the area. Traditional sheep herders graze their flocks on juniper saplings to keep a balance between heath and low growing trees. To

47

this day, they follow the animals across the land, spinning and knitting lambs' wool while they walk. This biosphere of honey, meat, and wool production gives the area an almost mystical atmosphere.

Celle city's charter dates back to the 13th century. Old city views show a fortified stronghold on the Aller River. A castle on a hill, surrounded by a moat and park, a knights' tournament square, and an imposing church still form the center of town. Street names bring the guild system of past ages to the pres-

The Welfen Castle in Celle became the residence of the Royal House of Hanover, and was the birth place of King George III. After World War II, the castle housed art treasures retrieved by the Monuments Men.

ent: North and South Wall, Fishermen's Gate, Tax Collectors' Street, Shoemakers' Lane, Holy Cross. In the Middle Ages, Celle belonged to the powerful Guelph/ Welfen Dynasty. Disputes over the priceless "Guelph Treasure" of medieval Christian art have surfaced in 2014. This treasure was purchased in 1935 from Jewish art dealers for the Berlin museums, possibly under Nazi duress.

Ornate 16th Century Building.

The city's half-timbered houses were ornately carved and painted in bright colors with biblical inscriptions, flowers, 16th century dates, and even portraits and names. A favorite decoration with the children was the *Dukatenmännchen:* it showed a long tailed creature relieving himself of gold coins into a chamber pot. There were real stocks and neck irons for thieves in back of the town hall. I imagined the good townspeople kicking and spitting at chained evildoers.

Auguste's favorite meat market Matthies advertized beef and pork—R*ind und Schweine Schlachterei.* I held on tightly to her hand; I had read *child and pig slaughterhouse,* and feared that Herr Matthies was coming after me with his hatchet.

Historically, Celle was connected in Personal Union to the British Throne and other European courts by the 18th century. The district's High Court and a Royal horse breeding farm had been gifts to the city by the English King George II in 1711. Still in existence during the war, the stud farm raised stallions for equestrian SS officers.

By an even older ordinance, the Hanover area once maintained a strict system of eleven social classes.

Narrow Street and St. Mary's Church.

These layers of authority and respect for judges, jurists, advocates and law clerks had created a climate of high standards in spite of an easy, rather sleepy conservative mentality.

The young Prince George of Hanover, born at Celle Castle, was to become King George III, the hated foe of the American Revolution. Like his father George II, King George III graciously offered a choice of royal gifts to his two favorite towns, Göttingen and Celle: a university, or a penitentiary. Folklore maintains that Celle's city fathers picked the latter option. A safe house would be far better than an academic institution with wild young men, always drunk, in debt, and set on ruining the local women's virtues, they argued. The modern traveler, arriving by train, finds a handsome Baroque palace close by the railway station—King George III's prison, still in use today, modernized and fortified. Indeed, the city was rich in history. King George's other gift in Göttingen was to become my Alma Mater.

Queen Caroline Mathilda, sister of George III, was beloved in town. Her tragic life and legend were still taught in grade school, appropriately modified. At thirteen, she was married to the young and mentally unstable King Christian VII of Denmark who entrusted all matters of governance to his progressive royal physician.

Count Struensee, the doctor, came from the Hamburg area, which was then part of the Kingdom of Denmark. Under the doctor, Denmark became a most enlightened and modern state, practicing all the ideas of equality, liberty, and human rights that the French Revolution would proclaim decades later. Danish reactionary Protestant forces caught on in shocked disapproval.

When an affair between the Queen and the doctor was discovered, he was arrested. His nude body was publicly dismembered in Copenhagen, then beheaded and quartered. The Queen was forced to watch the execution before she was exiled in her native Celle castle. She lived in the castle from 1772 to 1775, attended to the poor and sick until she was poisoned by Danish spies. Mystery and intrigue from long ago accompanied these stories.

Connections to the former Kingdom of Hanover and the British Empire still existed. A British Hanoverian regiment had been garrisoned in Celle up to 1866, when the city fell under Prussian administration. The pride of the city museum was a large hall decorated with victorious scenes of various British battles. Showcase after showcase paraded historical red British uniforms. A few families in town could trace their ancestry to the British and other Royal Houses, but during the Third Reich these families kept silent about their foreign connections.

Oma's house and garden, and the city of Celle left indelible impressions on me.

We had arrived in Celle in the spring of 1943. I attended the near-by grade school for a short while before the summer break. It was obvious that I had learned very little in Berlin, I could not even write my own name.

The principal was a most serious supporter of the Führer. Every morning started with a ceremony under the Swastika flag in the school yard. We sang *HJ* songs and raised our right arms for the *Heil Hitler* greeting. Should a pupil forget to greet the man properly somewhere in the hall or stairwell, he ordered the student to walk in front of him, shouting that greeting a hundred times with an extended right arm, while the principal counted...*eins...zwei...drei...vierzig.....achtundneunzig.*

And again, there were the obligatory trash collecting requirements and air raid drills or times of "blind alarms" when we had to run home. Old Herr Schuhmacher, our second grade teacher, had come out of retirement at a time when younger teachers were at the front. I recall the bizarre image of this long-legged man, dressed in black and with a violin under his arm running home as we children did.

The school also had a shelter dug into an adjoining old cemetery. We sat on rough wooden benches with the cold soil in our backs and scared each other with horror stories of skeleton hands grabbing us, and skulls rolling under our feet.

After school was out for the summer, Mutti enrolled me in a day camp. When I talked about my first day there, Mutti saw to it that I never went back. The camp teacher had commented on my blond braids and announced that I looked just like a little girl that would hand flowers to Herr Hitler, if he ever came to town.

For the remaining weeks of that wonderful summer of 1943, I played in Oma's house and garden with my neighborhood friends Ilse, Marlies, Ursula, Inge, and Brunhilde, who all wanted to come to our garden. Their mothers worked in war related industries, and all their fathers were in the army. Mutti spent her time as a Red Cross nurse at the train station, attending to the needs of traveling children and men in uniform.

We girls innocently played a game that clearly expressed Nazi thinking. We drew a circle in the sand, with a smaller circle—Germany—in the center. Arbitrary country borders were drawn into the space between the circles: England, Poland, France, Russia, or whatever came to our minds. We stood around the circle, holding hands.

One of us called out: *"Ich habe Wut auf das verdammte Land Polen."* (I am furious at damn Poland). Then we girls would pull and shove until one stepped on Poland. Now that player was out, and Poland's border was connected to the German space at the center. More pushing, and more countries were incorporated into the German Reich. Perhaps we had learned this game in school. How ironical that these fantasies of German invasions and propaganda for a glorious final victory were all drawn in the sand.

I was now left to Oma's care for this splendid summer. Oma, our maid Martha, the very old gardener Herr Herring, and I tended to the house and garden, but there was plenty of time for exploring. Today, it is hard to imagine the amount of physical work that a household required, and an old fashioned one like ours in particular.

Laundry was especially hard work. In the washhouse, a fire burned under the copper tub that was encased in masonry work. After considerable time of heating, our linens, towels and personal items boiled in the soapy water. When the fire was low and the water had cooled down, the heavy wash was lifted out, wrung and rinsed, and carried to the courtyard. It was my job to place the laundry poles into sunken metal retainers and pull the clothesline from pole to pole. Martha hung the wet laundry out to dry. All of this was very demanding physical work. I learned to ride Mutti's bicycle between billowing sheets, holding on to the laundry poles.

We knew no conveniences and did not miss what we had never dreamed possible. With an established work ethic, life ran smoothly. But it was essential to have a maid. Martha had been in the family for quite a long time. Oma encouraged a romantic liaison between Martha and a stable hand from King George's old stud farm. I was told to sit with the two as a chaperon when they whispered over a beer in the kitchen. He expressed his appreciation by delivering a few loads of fresh horse manure from the stables for Oma's flowerbeds and vegetable garden.

The house still exuded an air of Oma's grand time in London. She had kept Opa's library with all the heavy bookcases and a billiard table. Among his books were beautifully illustrated botanical volumes, German literary classics, and a set of Dicken's novels, along with other English publications. I spread my Bakelite zoo animals all over the green felt of the billiard table, and, since the space was used by nobody else, I could leave my arrangements there for the longest time.

This great play station came to an end when Oma's youngest brother, a military physician, requested the billiard table for the officers' mess at the Russian front, where he, as head of staff, operated a field hospital and wanted traditional relaxation from the stress of war. Oma agreed and had the billiard equipment shipped to that distant land. On the final rushed retreat from Russia, both the billiard table and the doctor returned safely to his hometown. A good hundred years old by now, the table is still in the family.

Oma's sewing spot was an elevated throne surrounded by a banister of oak columns, overlooking the garden. Opa Karl's full size portrait smiled down at me; he wore a red vest with a gold watch chain. His mustache and glasses made him look like the American president Theodore Roosevelt, not at all like Kaiser Wilhelm with his upturned, waxed mustache.

Oma's large portrait hung in the dining room. With her loosely arranged hairdo and a flowing white voile dress she was a royal presence. There were other large

Oma Auguste's family treasure—a very old Chinese platter.

paintings of landscapes or mythological scenes. Suspended on the dining room's oak paneling, and somewhat out of place, was a rather large Chinese plate in pink and green glaze from Auguste's family. Broken, reassembled, glued, and held together firmly by metal clips, the plate was treasured by Auguste.

Hidden behind wood panels was a steel safe which housed Karl's extensive collection of Greek, Roman, and early regional German coins. At times, this fascination with Numismatics had angered Auguste who tended to be practical and penny pinching, and had little sense for the aesthetics of her husband's hobby. But Karl's collection retained its worth through several devaluations until it was split and sold in the 1970s.

The service wing included several storage rooms and a spacious kitchen. Dutch wall tiles, one even dated to the late 18th century, displayed skaters, fishermen, windmills and other scenes from Holland. Meticulously scrubbed floor tiles kept the kitchen clean and cool. There was no refrigeration. Eggs, milk, butter and cheese, meat, fruit, juices, jams and cakes were kept in the fruit cellar under the kitchen.

A white enamel sink hung in the far corner, connected to water pipes on the outside of the house. The sink was suspended on the wall with a large splash board behind it. It had one cold water spigot and drained from a tub that looked like a fully rounded stomach. The dish washing equipment occupied one whole wall of the kitchen: a long table with two sunken tubs, one to be filled with hot water from the stove for washing and scrubbing, the other one with cold water for rinsing. When finished, the tubs with dirty water were lifted up, carried across the kitchen, and dumped into the sink.

The stove was a huge, tiled wood and coal burning monster with iron rings on the cooking surface that were removed or added to accommodate different pot sizes over the flames. Large cabinets held culinary wonders and dishes of all sizes and purposes. I remember to this day the smell of bay leaves, picked from a garden shrub and stored in a big pillowcase in the kitchen cabinet.

Set off in one corner was a pantry full of baskets and very old storage tins. I loved looking at the decorative pictures on these tins from the former colonies in Africa and China, with elephants and camels and natives working under coconut trees.

A large wood table in the middle of the kitchen served for all activities: cutting vegetables, rolling out pastries, gutting chickens, preparing fruit for canning, larding meat roasts, eating, and for me in grade school, doing home work. The kitchen had remained unchanged for a good forty years.

In the winter, the water needed to be turned off every night to prevent pipes from freezing and bursting. This process required crawling into the dark cellar under the kitchen and fumbling to shut off the main water line, then running through the house, shouting instructions, turning all faucets on to let all remaining water run out of the pipes, and then reversing the whole drama the next morning. Buckets of water supply stood around in case the day temperature was too cold to turn the system back on the next morning.

House and garden in Celle, 1910. An air raid bunker was constructed on the middle level in 1943.

The garden had been Opa Karl's passion. Descending in three terraces from the solarium to the lowest level, the garden offered a view beyond the property to a park, over meadows and the Aller River. The top level was supported by a brick wall and offered a showy presentation of flower beds lined with boxwood. A Greek urn, a five sided sun dial, a grotto for afternoon *Kaffee*, a stone cannon ball, and a bird bath adorned the arrangements.

A central path led to a wide set of steps on the middle level. Here were picturesque sitting areas under an ash tree, lawns, and more flower beds. The curving stairs down on either side of this sitting group were made of alpine Dolomite stone and offered pocket beds for Karl's rock gardening.

The lowest level was designed as a utility garden with its rows of beans, leeks, carrots, peas, rhubarb plants, herbs and berry bushes. A small pond and a two story garden pavilion provided much interest. Throughout the garden, Karl had planted orchard specimen of rare fruit trees and espaliered grapes grew along the house.

There were endless opportunities for play. Martha had obtained bunnies to fatten up for a good winter roast. Feeding and stroking the bunnies was fun, and they actually laid colored eggs at Easter. Placed in an enclosure that could be moved, they nibbled the grass and kept the lawn short and fertilized without mowing.

Toys were no longer available in the stores, but we did not need new ones anyway. The old sheds held play things from our mother's childhood; a red, wrought iron sled in the shape of a chair, a baby bed with a torn canopy, carts, and parts of Mutti's book binding press. Her midwife's medical satchel was there with a forceps and other implements, along with Karl's apothecary scales and weights. The trunk full of costumes delighted the neighborhood friends and me endlessly.

On the lowest garden level, a very tall, hollow linden tree had been cut down for fear it might fall on the tea house pavilion. The tree's center hole was large enough for us to crawl through and send all sorts of things down the tunnel. There were endless hours of play around the pond with its tadpoles and dragonfly larva. The apple trees and berry bushes provided enough snacks.

The garden pavilion was mysterious. It sat elevated on airy storage space and had just one room upstairs, surrounded by windows on all sides. In it, one

was a little closer to the tree tops and the clouds. Vagrants had broken in and set up residence for a few days. It was locked afterwards. We climbed the external stairs and looked in through the window panes, but playing there was forbidden.

Oma was a firm believer in physical exercise for children. Over the years, she had bought a set of parallel bars for her various grandchildren, along with a high jump installation, height-adjustable stilts, and a swing set with rings, a trapeze, a bar, and a rope ladder. The parallel bars were made of polished oak that rested in heavy wrought iron fittings. It took extra efforts to move the thing out of storage in the former horse stables. The garden and this sports equipment guaranteed us hours of fun.

Owing to her interest in exercise, Oma would walk me to gym classes at the Men's Sporting Association and stayed to observe the activities. The children rotated from ladders to parallel bars to rings, to floor exercises with hoops and balls. The padding on the floor was sawdust and it got into everything: our balloon-like pants, hair and ears and nostrils and it itched. But it absorbed shocks and was fun to kick around with our bare feet.

Auguste sat like a silhouette in the spectator's gallery, wearing her black dress and veiled hat, and watched the yelling mass of children down below. Afterwards, she examined me thoroughly for sawdust, shaking out my braids and my shirt, and making me turn the elastic band around my balloon–pants legs inside out. Then we had real ice cream from an Italian vendor with a very non-German name like Pellegrini or Tontonelli in his cafè, where we admired cakes and tortes made with rare butter, cream, eggs and flour.

The summer seemed like one eternally warm play period for me. There were few air raids during the day. If an alarm sounded at night, all residents assembled down the steep staircase into the dank fruit cellar: the von Schluters, the teacher, Martha, Oma, Mutti and I. We sat on the stairs and on potato bins. There was no space for other seating arrangements. But then, in August of that year, our Berlin apartment was hit.

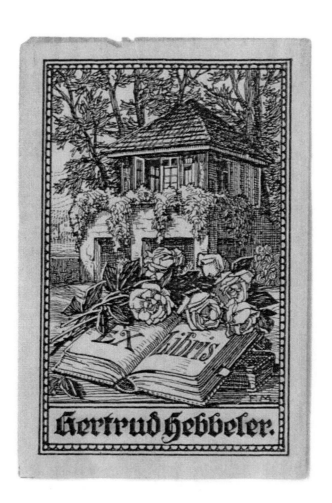

Ex Libris

Gertrud Hebbeler.

Mutti worried about our family's safety under the increasing air strikes. Vati was still in Berlin. Arend, now barely 16 and his entire class formation had been sent to *Arbeitsdienst*, the mandatory work service, which had evolved into military service. He and his friends were stationed in Stettin at the Baltic coast and were trained as anti-aircraft gunners. They attended school in the morning and manned their guns at night, deadly tired and frightened.

Achim remained at Templin, rather lonely and feeling abandoned. He sent photographs of the school's performance of *Shakespeare's Midsummer Night's Dream*, holding a donkey's mask in his role as Nick Bottom. The school might well have taken a serious risk with this play, as all foreign cultural performances were forbidden—plays, films, concerts, art exhibits in favor of shallow Hitler Kitsch.

I remember that Mutti took me along for a concert in Celle's church. She probably did not want to leave me at home alone, and I was awed. As the former house of worship for the court, the church was richly decorated with painted galleries and religious statuary. I liked St. Peter the best with his large key to heaven. There was spooky funerary art with an old Duke and his Duchess praying on a pile of skulls. A gilded balcony had been the seat for the prince and the court, and all the glamour of so long ago was still there.

The town had a long musical tradition. According to church records or folklore, even Johann Sebastian

Bach had visited on his travels and had played the organ in Celle. Ever since then, the rich musical heritage had been cultivated and appreciated. At this particular concert, the singers in their black robes and white collars transfixed me. I listened as their voices rose: first the men, then the women, then the increasing density of the musical texture. They sang words, a text, and I was amazed that the words did not become shouting, did not rub and bite each other. If we talked like that in school, we would be told to shut up. The harmony that I heard came from words, I thought, and it was the skill of the composer to find the right words that fit together.

The Bach Kantorei in Celle's Castle Chapel.

Then air raid sirens sounded into the performance and lights were turned off. The choir continued from memory. The congregation remained in their pews, anxiously listening to the noises of planes overhead in the stillness of contemplation and fear.

Mutti tried to carry on a life as normal as possible.

She oversaw my swimming instruction by the river. I wore an inherited, moth eaten wool swimsuit. Wet wool shrank, would not dry, and felt freezing cold in the mild climate of our summers. It was laborious to put on and pull off. During the lesson, I lay on my tummy in the grass and learned how to coordinate breast strokes with froggy leg movements. For the actual water tryout, Mutti had fashioned a vest from heavy old drapery material. Knowing that cork would float, she had sewn wine corks into a row of pockets around my waist. But the contraption did not work; the old wormy corks did not support me. I learned to swim anyway and spent countless hours on the river.

Celle, like all other cities, had mostly female residents since the men were at war. I cannot recall any fathers in my friends' families. The only two men that I remember were a friendly old cabinet maker in his sunny workshop, and Herr Herring, the gardener. We girls visited the old man and admired his craft with the lathe and saws in a place that smelled of carpenter's glue. The gardener was a World War I veteran from the Shelter for Homeless Men. Oma had allowed him to grow a few tobacco plants. He tended to them lovingly, stringing the leaves up in the fall to dry, along with stingingly smelling walnut leaves for his pipe. Herr Herring had survived a head injury that was still visible on his bald pate. Disrespectfully, Arend called it a thumbprint into the pale, risen dough of a loaf of yeast bread.

Mutti visited Vati a few times in the apartment in Berlin during the summer and experienced the aftermath of a bombing night, when the heat from burning buildings melted the asphalt in the streets, and explosive air pressure felt falsely like upcoming rain storms.

In the night of August 24, 1943, our apartment building in Berlin was bombed to the ground while all the residents sat in the shelter below, fearing for

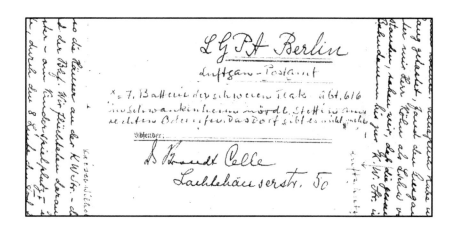

Vati's letter to Luftwaffenhelfer (anti-aircraft gunner) Arend, telling him of the bombing loss of our home, 1943.

their lives. Then they fled into the open as explosions continued and debris hurled about. My father wrote to his sons Arend and Achim to inform them of the loss of our home. His letters give a full account of the horrors of that night; they combine facts and amazing consolation. The letters are written in Vati's exacting hand writing, without any sign of a trembling hand, and yet one can feel how shaken he is. Both brothers carried their letters with them until they eventually found their way back to Celle. For that reason, I can quote from Arend's letter which he received while stationed with his flack unit on the Baltic:

Celle, 8-26-1943
My dear boy, our beautiful home is no more. But I, and we all, must deal with this loss. You too will overcome it. You have lost many beautiful things-books, and many items that you had collected and cared for. But it can all be replaced. You and we all still have a home with your grandparents in Celle and Dissen. Let us be grateful to God that He protected and saved me in this ordeal, and that we can all stay to-

gether. When you think this through, you will be able to deal with this loss. I am thankful that none of you saw these hours of horror.

Good bye, my dear boy, take heart and be brave. You can see that God has been at our side in this great danger. I send you my love, your father.

The letter provides a chilling account from ground level. Vati describes how he as the air warden directed the others out of the cellar in the dark, through smoke and dust and shrapnel on rehearsed escape routes, holding on to a few valued belongings. Vati ventured back into the smoldering cellar after the occupants had made their way out. He felt his way along the walls until he found those two cases that Mutti had packed, and he managed to lift them through the escape hatch.

In the flying debris he stumbled into the splinter ditch running the length of our building. From there he watched the unthinkable inferno of flames devouring all we owned; every house on the street was furiously burning. Since all buildings stored coal in large bins in the cellars, fires intensified with this fuel and could not be put out by the bursting water pipes. He described how the glowing steel beams in the building melted and bent and crashed into the rubble piles. A bomb had hit the far end of the protective ditch, killing eight people. Soup was supplied by the Red Cross. He spent a day and two nights in the ditch until the dangers from late exploding bombs subsided and he could walk through the burning city to reach relatives, lugging his two suit cases along. A few hours of talking, rest, a bath and a clean shirt was all they had to offer.

After serious air attacks, the German postal service mailed free information cards across the country to indicate peoples' survival. That was how Mutti knew that Vati would come to Celle once the trains operated again. He arrived a few days after the Berlin trauma. When she picked him up at the station—a broken man, his wife dead, his sons at war, his home gone up in flames, his father recently deceased, his brothers killed—she decided that Wilhelm needed a wife, and we three children a real mother. Trude could provide what little stability there was in the house in Celle, and they would marry. After all, we had long formed very strong family ties.

I see my father in the living room, tired, emaciated and somber. He wears ill fitting, old fashioned clothes on loan from Herr von Schluter. The stiffly starched shirt collar surrounds his neck like a white wall, and the old fashioned boots can barely be laced up tightly enough. He reports that the two heavy suit cases are safely watched over by friends. Then he unpacked one last item from our burnt-up home: a soup ladle from the kitchen, the only thing he could find in the smoldering ruins. It was bent and twisted from the heat, the light blue enamel had cracked off in places. We kept this ladle from the Berlin kitchen in the Celle kitchen for thirty years. It hung with other gadgets on a utensil rack like a sacred victim among its shiny new siblings.

Vati had only a few days of rest with us before he needed to return to his post in Berlin, and to more nights of bombings. Back in Berlin, Vati applied for permission to relocate his family in Celle and have ration cards transferred.

Three official forms were needed: a permit to leave Berlin due to homelessness, a permit to live in Celle, and a *Versorgungsnachweis*/Entitlement to receive provisions in a new location. *(See images on pages 68 and 69).*

Both my brothers remember the shock of losing their childhood home with all their treasures and memories of happy times. With Arend drafted into military service, Achim was desperately lonely in his boarding school and felt deep sadness over his burnt up home. He was not supposed to share his feelings—it just was not done, and other boys had received even worse news. To this day, I do not remember that feeling of loss. I was in Celle, Mutti and Oma cared for me

there, I had my white dream bed, my dolls, and house and garden for playing.

A few letters from Vati's mother also survived and express her raw emotions over her son's near death experiences. Worried and practical, she then inquired about Vati's underwear size, hoping that she might be able to purchase the items, provided that he could send his clothing coupons.

Vati's story made Oma decide that a shelter needed to be available with better access and that the Kohlmeiers should be included as well. With this in mind, she contracted with a local carpenter and had a bunker

built under the lawn on the middle terrace. Benches lined the sides along support timbers in the cold garden soil. An emergency exit tower at the far end provided a wooden escape ladder. A heavy door was installed to keep animals and rain out, but it was damp, and puddles of water accumulated after all. Even for me, life was becoming more serious, and the bunker was not a happy place for play. I am not sure that the structure would have been strong enough to save lives. And Oma in her long black dress would never have crawled out of this trap.

I remember many nights when we sat in the bunker, shivering, and waiting out the air raids in the region. The bunker was bitterly cold in the dampness of winter. Sirens sounded different levels of urgency: early warning, take cover, and immediate danger. We knew what the howling sounds meant. In a quiet summer night, the sirens also awakened animals and wild-life—dogs barked, roosters crowed, ducks quacked, birds shrieked, and frogs croaked by the river; nature felt diffused fear.

All residents in the house would stumble in with their valuables. I had a backpack with my teddy bear Seppi, the Kohlmeiers brought their bedding, our elegant friends from upstairs brought their treasures in a large hat box. On the muddy floor, the cardboard box soaked through and all the sterling flatware tumbled to the soggy floor. It was a scene of comic relief in the anxiety of the night. The teacher had moved on. Her third floor apartment was now occupied by Herr and Frau Esser, who had recently arrived from Holland. The Essers were loyal Hitler supporters and had feared that the advancing Western Allies might not be friendly to them, and that a return to the Reich was a safer choice. Down in the bunker, Herr Esser fervently proclaimed his faith in the Führer and foretold Germany's final victory over all enemies.

One night stands out in my memory. In the flak search lights overhead, we realized that the planes were flying south, leaving our city undisturbed. We stepped out of the bunker and watched the frightening drama in the night sky. Hanover was thirty miles to the south, making the city's war related industries there a bombing target. The first advancing planes were night scouts. We could see from below how they dropped flares to mark the target areas—*Christmas trees* we called those evil lights in desperate sarcasm.

Bomber planes followed and unloaded explosives over the city. With the next formation of planes came incendiary phosphorous bombs which intensified the fires down below. With this combination of explosive- and fire bombing, whole city areas could be annihilated with the effect of carpet bombing. Even over the distance, it was noisy, and we had learned to interpret the sounds—different planes, distance of detonations, drones.

Across the flat lands, fires from the burning city of Hanover blazed into the night sky in bright yellow, red, and orange, and clouds of dust and smoke darkened the sun rise for the following days. Our Aunt Annie lived there, and we were worried about her safety. Oma declared that the British would never bomb us, they liked gardens and lawns, and we were fine in our garden bunker. Indeed, Celle was spared; it was not an important target. Only a few last bombs fell two days before the city surrendered.

Towards the end of 1943, Martha was recruited under her loud protests to work as a seamstress in a uniform factory. Like all other women, Aunt Annie in Hanover had also received orders to sew for a military plant. Mutti's work at the train station exempted her from factory work. Being without a maid, working, and taking care of an aging mother and a young child allowed her to obtain domestic help. Mutti was notified that she had been granted an official permit for a foreign maid. A neighbor received similar information. Another note arrived, directing them to the employment office in December 1943 to pick up a girl from a shipment of women removed from German occupied Ukraine.

Mutti and our neighbor took our hand-pulled wooden cart along and set out across town. After hours of waiting, open trucks arrived and females wrapped in blankets were unloaded in turmoil and confusion. A sergeant barked out German names and assigned a foreign woman in line to each family.

That's how two Ukrainian girls in slave labor lived next door to each other in war time Celle, and how we became friends with Marusja. Her belongings consisted of cloth bundles tied into a metal tub. All was loaded on Mutti's cart and hauled home through the cold night. Marusja was to sleep in one of the storage rooms by the kitchen. She pulled her few items into the house and began to unpack the fur bundles from the tub—and out came a baby.

"*Lida, Lidotshka*" her mother sang to the baby and held her close. We did not speak each other's languages. We wondered if Marusja had given birth to this tiny miracle on the enforced, freezing trek westward, and had cleverly provided for food in a sturdy tub that could glide over ice and snow. Bags of dry beans, buckwheat and salt surrounded the baby. The little girl peeled out of her warm wrappings, was pink and well and happy. Oma Auguste looked at the strangers. "You are the salt of the earth" she quoted from the Sermon on the Mount.

The Ukraine had been a powerful nation in ancient times. Her central location, oil fields and rich agrarian lands caused incessant warfare with Russia, Poland, Austria, and Germany. Ukrainian culture and language were severely suppressed when the country became a founding Republic in the Soviet Union in 1922. Nazi troops occupied the country in 1941 during the Russian offensive. With the German labor force fighting or working for war industries, it had become common practice in the Third Reich to force residents from occupied lands to work as slave laborers in Germany. The men frequently worked in urban sites on the removal of debris and unexploded bombs. Domestic service for women was the better place.

Our family now consisted of Oma Auguste, Mutti, Marusja, the baby, and me. Mutti applied for food and clothing ration cards for the newcomers. On all official business, Mutti fought the same battle with officials that she was not an enemy spy, despite her London birthplace. Every single item for purchase was rationed now. There was much work in house and garden. Marusja knew how to peel potatoes, do the laundry, and sweep the floor. I learned to hold and clean and feed little Lidotshka and take her for walks in a borrowed stroller.

Marusja was almost a kid like I was. She discovered the joys of western civilization: a vacuum cleaner, a flushing toilet to be operated endlessly, a piano that sounded so glorious when she sat on the keys, and spring upholstery that sent her flying up in the air. Oma taught us to knit. We helped in the kitchen together, with sign language for communication.

In anticipation of the winter and possible food shortages, we canned fruit and sliced carrots and apples for drying. Marusja and I picked nuts from the big walnut tree by the house. Sometimes we climbed on the low roof overhang and poked the nuts out of the gutters. Still in their green coats, the nuts dried on wire racks with gunny sack covers to keep the squirrels out. We fed green beans into a slicing machine and packed the lot in salt in Opa Karl's tall water filtering containers. We cut acidic rhubarb sticks and pushed them into sterilized wine bottles for winter storage. Apples and pears were harvested and carefully sorted and stored in the cellar, or peeled and sliced to be dried. Fallen fruit was loaded on the hand cart and rolled to the cider press in town.

Mutti began to make other preparations for the worst hard time to come. She filled several shopping bags in easy reach with dried fruits and vegetables and whatever else could be spared from the meager daily rations. Warm clothing was packed along with it. These were bare essentials to carry with us if need be. She picked a spot in the garden on the second level by the central steps and dug valuables into the ground. Another hideout for her father's coin collection was dug into the ground of a shed, under the fire wood.

Back in Berlin, Vati was dispatched to find a new location for the fire damaged Department of Agriculture. His familiarity with land estates made him the right man for this task. The order instructed him to find suitable housing for all colleagues and staff members, but not for their families. Files, archives, and correspondence were to arrive later by train. On an exploratory trip, carrying his few belongings and the two cases with him, Vati found an estate to the south east of Berlin in Silesia and gave instructions for the move, but his plan was to move closer to Celle.

The wedding, (front row) grandmothers, Christiane, right: Arend, a widowed aunt, Achim, Vati, Mutti and other relatives, October 1943.

In the midst of all the chaos of war, Mutti made preparations for Vati's and her wedding festivities as one last good family event. The house was polished and shined up, draperies washed, china came out of storage, the garden weeded and raked. Women had developed singular skills in bartering, and Mutti was no exception. "A lace tablecloth for a few bottles of wine?" "Real coffee and butter for a first edition of Goethe, the 19th century national poet?"

74

Vati, the bridegroom, arrived in high spirits, off for a few days from his new location with the evacuated Department, the boys came on furlough, and I had shocked my teacher with an innocent "my parents are getting married." Relatives came and brought soup chickens for the wedding feast, real cakes were baked, and the weather was glorious.

On the evening before the wedding, neighbors participated in a noisy *Polterabend*. This tradition obligated the groom to help with the housework: guests and friends smashed bottles and crockery on the steps by the front door for Vati to clean up. I had learned a little poem and delivered my gifts, looking like a country girl: a basket of wooden cooking spoons, not that there was much food for cooking. Wedding presents arrived that seemed utterly useless, like large paintings and delicate crystal wine decanters and goblets. These items were probably obtained in the private bartering system as well, since shops no longer sold such merchandize.

Horse-drawn carriages from King George's stud farm took us to church where I had the important duty of flower girl. And then the guests dined in Oma's splendid house as if there were no worries in the world. It was a wonderful day in late October 1943.

Vati returned to his new place of work in Silesia. The memories of the wedding and the joyous family gathering sustained him while he explored the dreary country location. Several letters to Mutti described his new environment, I quote one source:

Wülschkau, 12-7-1943
I arrived after 30 hours of train travel. My colleague, Dr. M. arrived shortly after I got here. We were met by an elderly stenographer who had brought a handcart for our luggage. It took us two hours to get to the

Wülschkau "Castle" housed the evacuated Department of Agriculture from Berlin and a group of 40 Hitler Youth boys.

"castle," which was built some 30 years ago by a pretentious admiral; it is surrounded by a nice park.

The building is spacious, but we have only a few cold rooms because the Hitler Youth— about 40 boys of 9-11 years and their teachers have taken all the rooms with the warm southern exposure. I share a room with Dr. H.; it is very sparsely furnished. My bed has a thin straw mattress and one blanket. We were told that the new man of the National Socialist Movement needs no pillows, no sheets or blankets as they weaken one's character. The new man sleeps flat on his back and is hard and strong. I had not received this directive when leaving Berlin. However, older men may have a small pillow. Perhaps you could give me a sofa pillow when I come at Christmas? But then, I doubt that travel permits will be granted for the holidays.

Hitler Youth groups had been quartered in the castle in Celle as well. HJ flags hung from the windows of the Renaissance building and the boys' presence

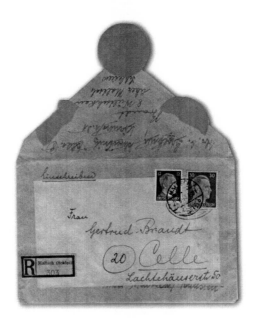

Lack of supplies—Vati reused a colleague's envelope to write to Mutti in Celle.

was evident at parades and special ceremonies. Where did they come from? They had been displaced and removed from their parents and from bombing dangers in large cities. Did they go to school in the castle? Did they practice marching in military formation in the castle's inner court yard? Their stories were like those my brothers experienced.

Shortly before Easter 1944, Achim arrived for his confirmation service in Celle. Vati, Arend, and other relatives joined us for a short visit. Achim had received his Lutheran instructions in Templin under the predecessor of Pastor Merkel, the father of Germany's current chancellor Angela Merkel.

Marusja understood the event to be a religious celebration, perhaps she was a Russian Orthodox Christian herself, and Easter would be her High Holy Feast. *Arim, Arim confirmazi, confirmazi,* she said, along with *babushka boom, boom, babushka boom, boom* when she saw overhead enemy planes. We assumed that her grandmother had been a victim of German air attacks. For the celebration she baked traditional cakes for Achim, filled with the white beans that she had brought with her from Ukraine.

Mutti and my brothers had shown me how to read maps at an early age. It was easy to locate Germany in the middle of Europe, with the Atlantic and Baltic, with England and the Scandinavian countries to the North, Poland, Ukraine and Russia to the East, Austria to the South East, Italy and Switzerland to the South, France and the Netherlands to the West.

I could connect stories with these countries: Oma growing up near Denmark, the grandparents in England, Mutti traveling there and in Italy, grandfather Karl's picture postcards from Budapest and Prague with his filter demonstrations, my parents having lived on the Polish border before I was born, Oma's brother and other family members in Russia.

But now there were serious reasons to trace locations on the map with my fingers. Vati, Arend and Achim were in harm's way somewhere far from home. Two cousins served on submarines in the Atlantic, Aunt Annie's husband was stationed in France, her son was in Russia, and so were two other cousins and an uncle, and a friend fought with the doomed army division in Stalingrad. A good friend of Mutti's fought with Rommel's army in Africa, and where was Marusja's family in the Ukraine?

Achim had taught Mutti to decode some of the military broadcasts in order to be warned of enemy flight

78

patterns. It was now the summer of 1944. Achim and his school friends, in HJ uniforms and armed, had been transported out of the country for the duration of their summer vacation. They were under orders to dig pits along the Polish and Russian borders. But where were they? The propaganda merry-go-round still declared non-stop on the official radio station that digging trenches to trap advancing Soviet tanks, if they should ever come, was the teenagers' sacred duty.

We women were by ourselves again: Oma, Mutti, Marusja, the baby, and I. Household duties, staying warm, standing in line for food, mending our clothing, reading maps for bombing patterns, trying to decode radio messages, getting up with nightly air raids, waiting for mail, observing black-outs every evening, occasional school attendance, and hearing reports about increasing homelessness consumed our time. The business of staying alive was a full time occupation for civilians.

Vati had time to write reports from Wülschkau, where administrative work was impossible in the general chaos. Food for the Hitler Youth boys and his colleagues there consisted mostly of a few slices of bread with jam, and cabbage soup. Under these degrading conditions, his letters speak of his gratitude to his wife, who holds the family together and gives him the strength to continue in the nightmare of events. Long letters indicate that there is nothing to do for him but write, however:

Wülschkau, 11-5-1944
Today all the colleagues in the Department were mustered into the Volkssturm, the peoples' storm troopers, all grandfathers. I stood next to the local baker and his 15 year old apprentice, who had somehow managed to stay in town. Our company may be de-

tailed for training in Breslau in the next few weeks. Could you please find me a belt for my uniform pants? If you should still have any real string, <u>please, send it.</u> I need it for the pair of tough, used boots that make marching drills impossible without shoe laces. Also, please use my ration coupons for darning wool and send it as soon as possible, my socks have holes.

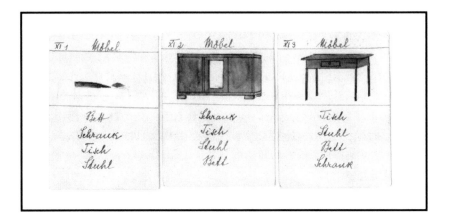

My father's hand-made card game, a birthday present.

Vati saved a letter from me after my birthday in November 1944. I filled two pages in pitiful spelling with a report about my birthday presents. I thanked him for the card game he made on blank army postcards. He had drawn familiar items in sets of four: the castle in Celle, the town hall, the church, and Oma's house; the set of furniture included a table, a bed, a cabinet, and a chair.

My letter documents the state of the economy, where hand-me-downs were the currency. In the absence of anything to buy, my friends brought me fistfuls of money, I reported 44 Reichsmark. Oma Clara sent a gold watch chain from her husband that I could wear as a necklace. Oma Auguste gave me two fragile, very thin china cups. Aunt Annie made a neat velvet dress with butterflies embroidered over moth holes and Mutti had talked Herr Esser into getting a doll bed made. Herr Esser was a guard in King George's historic penitentiary, and the bed came from the prison wood shop.

My favorite doll Heidi was sleeping in that bed, but she had changed into a boy, in a little lederhosen-like suit that Mutti had knitted. Heidi was now Achim and I hated the sex change. Achim became Heidi again, real fast. Mutti also traded some books for me with signatures of owners I did not know. It was a fantastic birthday!

In the evenings, Marusja and her neighbor friend sang melancholic Russian songs. They had now been with us for over a year, and the baby had grown. Marusja's husband Havriel/Gabriel came for a visit in the early spring of 1945 from his forced labor job of detonating unexploded air raid bombs in the streets of Hamburg. One spring morning Marusja, the baby in the stroller, and the neighbor girl disappeared for good. Had they heard of Germany's forthcoming collapse, and did they join up with the men? Did they try to walk back to their land? Did they become partisans? Or did partisans murder them for having worked for the German enemy? We would never find out. Marusja's tub remained behind and hung in our bathroom until the house was sold many years later.

In March 1945, when Achim had turned 15, he and his class mates were drafted. They escaped SS recruitment by mustering as applicants for Reserve Officer training. A year's schooling was scheduled, but the boys were sent east within a week. Mutti did not know if the boys had received any training for handling their guns and ammo, or where they had been deployed. Achim was frightened to his core. He had experienced paramilitary life the summer before, on his digging "vacation" with the HJ.

Imminent final victory was still proclaimed on the NSDAP broadcast network. To achieve victory, Hitler's Minister of "People's Enlightenment and Propaganda," Josef Goebbels, had asked on the radio:

"Do you want total warfare?" to which he had received a resounding "Yes" from the German population, or so it was reported. It is hard to imagine that anyone still believed these lies.

We knew from Vati's letters that Wülschkau was close to the advancing Soviet fighting line. Mutti preserved his letters from the last days of the war. Known as a diplomatic negotiator, my father was ordered to find yet another location for the truncated Department and archives in early 1945.

Vati and his colleagues were all in their fifties. Without a doubt, an open protest against this nonsense would have landed the men on the fighting fronts. The orders required them to stay in the general area of Berlin in the German North. Vati knew that their present location would soon be under Soviet control, according to the Yalta Conference. This was reason enough to pick a new location close to what he assumed to be the American or British demarcation line in the very near future.

It was hoped that the Western Allies would provide a more decent and humane treatment for the defeated population than was feared of the Russians. He found a makeshift location in an historic abbey. Again, he moved those two suit cases with him and stored them with newly made friends. I include excerpts from letters that we siblings discovered after both parents had died.

Hamersleben, 2-15-1945

The order to move the Department again came ten days ago. It is absolutely impossible to find a location that is not packed full with refugees. But I did find the old abbey in H. with its beautiful cloisters that have not been bombed. The manor house has been unoccupied for several years and housed the church archives. Those I had moved to the abandoned Catholic Church, and that way we gained 10 rooms. The old central heating system still works. The National Socialist party has promised wooden beds with straw sacks and 10 mattresses for the oldest men among us. My colleagues will come in a few days, I am not sure that our files will get here. These arrangements required considerable travel around, but I hope that my vagabond life will end with this move. Greetings to you, my dear wife.

Five weeks later, he wrote a last letter from that location, just a few days before Germany surrendered:

Hamersleben, 3-29-1945

My dear Trude,

I am writing to you in hopes this letter will reach you. We have not received any mail in three weeks, and I hope you are in good health.

My foot infection is healing. Long rest periods have been beneficial for the inflammation of my pulled ligaments. The doctor said that I may walk again in a few days. Have you heard from the boys? I cannot imagine Achim in uniform; I hope he is in a tolerably good camp. I expect a letter from Arend after Easter.

The fighting lines are moving with uncanny speed ever closer to this place. How soon will they be in town? If we stay alive, hunger will take over. If you and I should be separated and you survive, you must try to reach clients of Berkefeld Filter abroad and plead for food. I cannot imagine what is ahead of us. The boys are both far away, and Christiane, the dear child—I spare myself further thoughts, it is too painful.

Perhaps I will be deployed with the storm troopers at the last minute. Although it would be sheer nonsense, I cannot discount that possibility. Whether I stay here or reach you on foot depends on the situation. Perhaps my colleagues and I will be arrested. But do not worry. Whatever will happen cannot be avoided and will have to be endured. At least I have a clean vest. Walking home will require food for many days. It is also possible that there will be a complete ban on travel. I cannot imagine how you will get along. But I am calmed by the thought that you are there, and anyway, we must recognize that we are under the care of God. The anniversary of dear Edith's death will be in a few days. It is now six years. I am sure you will go to the cemetery with flowers. I do hope your mail will arrive soon...My love to all of you,

Yours, Wilhelm.

Even today, with the horrors of the war long overcome, this letter moves me deeply. I cannot imagine Mutti's anxieties over the fate of the boys, and Vati, somewhere hurled into the general collapse at war's end.

On April 8, 1945, two days before Celle surrendered, the only serious Allied bombing attack occurred on our city.

The train station had been the target, but surrounding residences, the gas works, and the Trill cookie factory had been hit as well, exposing large amounts of sugar, flour, and condensed milk. My friend Ilse proudly showed me the baking treasures that her mother had scooped up in the strictly fenced off streets, surrounded by "Keep Out" signs. As we learned later, this sweet adventure covered up the city's most sinister event imaginable in a desperate, last attempt to enforce Nazi ideology.

THE UPSIDE DOWN HOUSE
IN CELLE 1945

The war was not officially over until the unconditional surrender in May. Celle surrendered unconditionally to the Allies on April 12, sparing the city all street fighting or damage to the castle and old town center.

Frightened, we stayed indoors. All routines would change now. The threat of nightly bombings was over, and there was the desperate hope that the men would come home. The anonymous enemy that we had feared in the air was now a reality on our very streets. How would we live? We had been their enemies. How would they treat us?

Oma, Mutti and I were sitting over our meager lunch when a loud clatter indicated that the front door and guard chain had been broken. A British soldier stood in the room, pointing his gun at us women.

We sat quietly, as if paralyzed. Fear took hold of us, we could not stir. He wanted a camera and motioned with his head, *go, move, get it.* Mutti finally stood up and went to fetch her Leica. Then she remembered that the camera was at the repair shop and she had a claim check somewhere. She found it. Would the threatening man accept her explanation? As she approached him, he had looked around our dining room, had seen grandmother Auguste's imposing portrait in her white garment, turned on his heels "Oh, the old Queen," and was gone.

Queen Victoria and our grandmother, what a fitting confusion! Her portrait had come to our rescue.

*Portrait of Oma Auguste as a young
wife, "the old Queen."*

Only later could we laugh at the ironies in the event.
Oma's new name stuck, but was only whispered behind her back.

A few days after this event, a military convoy
stopped in front of our house. An officer demanded
to inspect the house. Pleased with what he saw, he informed Oma that she and all other residents had two
hours to clear out, as this house was to be the official
residence for the commanding officer in town.

With no negotiations possible, Mutti rolled up our
blankets and provisions and set out to find a new place
to stay. While packing, she saw a soldier playing with
my gold necklace from Dissen, and Mutti bravely used
her English skills to ask if he would let go of it and

return it to her little girl. The soldier handed her the necklace, and I still have it.

A room for us women was offered by friends down the street, and I slept on a cot under the rafters in the attic. Bathroom privileges were shared with other residents, and a make-shift kitchen opened in the root cellar. Mutti created a hot plate with an upside-down electric iron, supported by two bricks, and we could heat water there during the one hour of electricity.

I explored the attic and learned to crawl out of the easement window. What luck and fun! I could sit high over the town with my bare bottom on the roof tiles and my dress spread around me, and pee into the guttering. No need to go down four flights of stairs and stand in line by the bathroom door!

Neighbors were informed of our new abode. We had no idea of the whereabouts of my brothers and father, but we hoped that Arend and Achim and Vati would come home, looking for us.

One afternoon in June 1945 a haggard, tall man in a long uniform coat stood in the cellar kitchen. It was my brother Achim, at 15 years of age, a man now, and released from a British open air POW camp along the Atlantic coast. Mutti knew that he and his classmates had been recruited in March for a year of officers' training in an undisclosed location. She also knew that the Allies were already in our country, advancing from the East and the West, leaving little space in between—the war would be over soon.

Now, after his return, Achim told us that he and his friends had all received uniforms, guns that they did not know how to use, ammunition and helmets, and within a week, were marched east from one location to the next, without rhyme or reason. After two months of these exhausting and futile exercises they heard of Hitler's suicide and were told to drop all heavy equipment and run for their lives in a westward direction, away from the advancing Red Army tanks. They ran across devastated lands and burnt villages in fear, hoping to escape before the Soviets caught up with them.

An American flag on the horizon directed them to an entrance point. Thousands of soldiers and refugees crowded and pushed through a narrow gate in mortal fear of being left behind on the wrong side, and that would mean immediate execution or transport back east. They could already hear the rattle of tanks in pursuit.

To their relief, American service men finally waved the men across the border to safety, all along the demarcation line, not just through the registration gate. Once inside, they were put again in marching formation "go west, go west, this area will be under Soviet control, head west." The men, tired and defeated, trotted across the Elbe River Bridge where on April 24, 1945 the famous hand shake between the Allies—East and West—took place.

On their march, the men finally reached the barbed wire enclosures of a large British-run POW camp along the Atlantic coast. In horror, Achim spoke of the filth and stench of thousands of men in the compound, cursing and shouting and relieving themselves wherever possible. Since the war had depleted food and finances in England and on the continent, the British authorities could barely sustain the camps. Prisoners broke through the wire barriers and roamed the land for food, forever hungry in this *Kahlfrassland* (greedy guts land).

After another six weeks, the younger POWs were lined up for dismissal papers. Achim claimed to be a farm worker and was sent on his way in June, only to come home to an occupied house—but he had finally found us. Then he told us a joke that had made the rounds among the men: if there should be a war between the West and the East, the soldiers would certainly fight with the Russian army because that way they would become AMERICAN POWs.

In the final days of the war, German soldiers on the eastern front gave themselves up to the Western Allies so that they would not fall into the hands of the Soviet Army. The fear was shared by the population in the eastern provinces, who fled by the thousands under extremely hazardous conditions in the cold winter of 1944/45. In addition, liberated camps of foreign workers and concentration camps opened their gates for inmates to leave. This enormous migration of hungry and desperate people needed to be brought under control in an effort to avoid the spread of diseases and violence.

More than 11 million Germans and foreign workers were taken prisoner by the Allies who were unprepared to handle sanitation and food for these masses. As make-shift measures, they corralled the prisoners in barbed wire open air enclosures in the countryside. The British tried to provide shelter in old barns and industrial sites, but prisoners rarely had tents or any form of protection from late snows and rains. They had neither clothing nor blankets. Needless to say, the mortality rate was high, given that large numbers of inmates were wounded or close to starvation on arrival.

Achim brought a passport photo of our older brother Arend whom he had seen in the encampment. Pictures commonly served as signs of survival. A worn-out, tired Vati found us in our new lodgings as well. Like all his colleagues, he had walked away from his obligations to the collapsed Third Reich. En route, and still near Soviet country, Vati came across a country train line that still operated.

However, passage on the train was controlled by the British and required an official English permit.

The station master spoke no English and did not understand his new duties. In a desperate effort to get away, Vati explained the English instructions in exchange for a hastily fabricated permit with smudged seals and stamps. The train took him in the direction of Celle; he walked the remaining distance.

The one room for Oma and Mutti at the neighbor's had two temporary sleeping surfaces, it now accommodated four persons with no sheets or towels, no clothing, and very little food.

Arend returned the following week and brought his friends Erich and Horst with him from the British POW camp. All three young men had been friends in Templin and had been stationed in the same anti-aircraft gunning outfit. Horst and Erich knew that their homes were now lost under Soviet control, and they had no communication with any surviving family members. Horst was proud of his aristocratic title which he had not been permitted to use under the Nazis.

The secretive cruelties of the Hitler Regime became obvious to the public when the British authorities turned a popular garden restaurant on the river, and near Oma's house, into a hospital station. The dance floors became dormitories for the ill and starving inmates from the close-by concentration camp Bergen-Belsen. The camp's name is familiar today, but was not yet known then. It was the camp where Anne Frank died of Typhoid fever. Bergen-Belsen was not an extermination camp, rather an overcrowded transition camp where illness and hunger took thousands of lives.

With the collapse of the Nazi state, the guards had opened the gates and fled. Anyone able to walk could leave, and Celle was the closest town. In my own memory, I see nightmarish figures in striped pajamas suddenly seeking their way through town. The British military government provided nursing care and proper nutrition.

But what I did not hear as a child in those days was the added Nazi brutality of the "rabbit hunt." The few bombs that destroyed the neighborhood of the Trill cookie factory and the gas works in the night of April 8, 1945, had actually also hit an inhumanely overcrowded train with inmates destined for Bergen-Belsen. For the night, the train had stopped next to an ammunition train. The bombs exploded both trains into a disastrous inferno.

The inmates who managed to escape in the general chaos were hunted down by SS guards, Gestapo officers, and members of the local Nazi NSDAP Party during the next two days. Caught internees were herded into a sports field at night. Thirty of them were executed on the spot for suspicion of looting. Of the assumed 4,000 Ukranian, Russian, Dutch, and French internees in this transport, 487 exhausted men and women survived the ordeal and were marched the 11 miles north to Bergen-Belsen on April 10, two days before the city's surrender, and five days before the camp was liberated by British and Canadian armies.

Various camps dotted the entire area of Germany in a controlled network of facilities for POWs, foreign laborers, or displaced persons. There were residence camps, women's camps, recuperation sites, or holding locations for exchange prisoners with German nationals incarcerated abroad. The extermination camps for "unwanted life" were located in the East, mostly in German occupied lands. Prisoners were constantly reassigned and moved from camp to camp. Belsen was the westernmost camp; it consisted of a number of subcamps and had been a military training facility long before the SS took it over.

If asked, the German population usually claimed

no knowledge of these camps. It is hard to believe that supply trains and covert activities would not have been noticed. Local farmers delivered foodstuffs and surely had their suspicions.

But in a dictatorship, fear of being reported, punished, or shipped to a camp is part of daily living. The railroad system transported prisoners to isolated entrances of camps. As one of the largest employers, German Reich Rail demanded strictest silence and secrecy from employees. It was best not to see, not to hear, not to think. After liberation, the Western Allies took steps to ensure that civilians saw the horrors of these camps. Reports exist of tours through Dachau and Buchenwald where residents of near-by cities saw mass graves and crematorium ovens.

A Celle Massacre Trial was held in December 1947. Of the 14 leaders of military and police personnel involved in the massacre, 7 were acquitted for insufficient evidence, 4 were sentenced to 4–10 years in prison, and 3 were sentenced to death. One death was overturned on appeal; the remaining 2 sentences were reduced to 15–20 years. The British military government issued clemency decrees for all remaining inmates. Celle has since honored the victims of that night with a memorial and with the reconstruction of an historical Synagogue. Like many other cities, Celle installed brass *Stolpersteine,* (stumble stones) in the pavement with names and dates in front of the victims' former houses.

With all the chaos in the last few months of the war, we did not go to school for the better part of 1945. In the summer, my grade school building was turned into a hospital, as infectious diseases of all kinds spread. Returning soldiers, homeless refugees, and the local population all needed medical attention. Like many friends, I contracted a skin infection that was treated with kerosene and left scars all over my legs. It seemed that from my knees downward I was forever wrapped in fabric strips with smelly medical lotions. The entire town smelled of Lysol, brought in by the British. It was an unfamiliar smell to us.

By the end of the summer in 1945, the commanding officer and his staff found a roomier, more modern villa than Oma Auguste's. Now an exchange of residences was ordered in short time. The British Command moved into the large villa, the owner's family was ordered to evacuate to our house, and we received permission to return as well.

The newcomers were the von Hodenberg family with 11 children. They had taken in the Blanke family who had lost their home in the cookie factory one-night bombing. The fathers were law partners, but Dr. Blanke had not yet returned from the war. Frau Blanke moved in with their 5 children, including baby Nellie, and a grandmother.

We, as the house owners, moved into two rooms with the eight members now in the family. In general, the house was undisturbed and still furnished as it had been before British occupancy. Somehow, the house adapted to this squeeze. The von Schluters upstairs returned as well and gave up rooms, the Essers were still on the third floor, and Mrs. Kohlmeier took in her parents, old Mr. and Mrs. Henke, who had survived the Hanover bombing.

I became good friends with three boys in the Blanke family who were about my age. The youngest von Hodenberg daughter, *Elfe,* who was appropriately named for her rank among the siblings, became my closest buddy. The new occupants came from Celle or close by and knew the local community. They looked at the present scramble as a very temporary measure, until more appropriate housing could be found. But that would not be possible for some time to come.

It was so crowded in the house that the men of our extended family all found spaces on an open sleeping porch of yet another neighbor. We had left the house a few weeks prior, just Oma Auguste, Mutti, and I. We returned with an additional five men: Vati, Arend and Achim, Erich and Horst, and there were all the other new occupants of the house. That summer, a caravan of all these residents walked to the hospital for immunization shots. Baby Nellie had contracted Diphtheria, and we all needed to take precautions. But little Nellie died before her father had ever seen her.

Celle was not very far from the Iron Curtain that separated western lands from Soviet control. The city's main buildings and homes had not been destroyed in the war and could accommodate newcomers. By municipal statistics, our city was one of the most overcrowded towns, growing in population from 17,000 to 55,000 in a few tumultuous years, and with hardly any new construction.

The city's housing authorities gave out local addresses to the newcomers in the endless stream of refugees. We were informed to take in a Mr. Eckhardt from the Polish border, and his girlfriend, Frau Umnus from the Czech region in the southeast. Their families had been located in camps and would join them later. Until then, the pair took up residence in the garden pavilion. There was no water and no electricity in the building. After having been in crowded refugee camps, this was a private place to stay, it was a warm summer, and other arrangements would be made later.

Frau Umnus' daughter and parents eventually arrived, sharing the pavilion, and Herr Eckhardt moved back in with his wife and their children. They all squeezed into the main house. Vati's widowed and homeless sister-in-law arrived with her two daughters, Helga and Erika, our cousins. Somehow Mutti placed them with us as well.

The Essers suddenly disappeared. His open support for the Nazis had been known in Celle, and the couple may have felt safer going underground somewhere else. Their rooms became available now to reshuffle the other occupants.

Every available house had to take in refugees who had lost their homes to bombs or evacuation. Fear of the advancing Russian troops sent people westward by trucks, by horse drawn carts, by trains and on foot, whatever mode of transportation could be found. In addition, German residents were expelled from lands that had fallen under Soviet control. And then there were the tens of thousands of bombed-out citizens. Refugees came with bare essentials of just a grip of clothing, perhaps with blankets and nothing else. Taking homeless people in became a problem for the locals to provide space, food, water, electricity, clothing, bedding, and sanitation.

Now, in the summer of defeat in 1945, Oma Auguste's house was turned upside down and inside out. The Allies required a complete inventory of all residents with birth dates, places of origin, and former occupations at the front door of each house. Our list showed the names of more than 50 occupants, almost all strangers. The list included all age groups, people from very different regions and distant lands speaking dialects we did not quite understand, a mixture of class and culture, of education and skill, but all in need of shelter.

More families lived in the house than keys were on hand. Just a few years back, each party in the house had their security key to the front door, three keys in total. New keys were not available: the steel industry was destroyed and there were no manufacturing supplies. With a strict locked-door policy, a new system of door signals was devised for our comings and goings.

A second list by the front door identified how to

use the bell: two rings for the Blankes, four rings for the von Schluters, seven rings for the Eckhardts. But with electricity rationed for much of the time, banging and shouting were the common ways of communication. Our rooms were closest to the front door, and we detested opening the door for the noisy occupants of the house. The system caused much friction. When the door bell worked, some jokers purposely sounded wrong signals, just to annoy the rest of the occupants.

During the war, services were generally available, if on a very limited scale. While food, fuel, and all merchandize were rationed in the Third Reich, the basic needs of the population were still met. The infrastructure of utilities, roads, postal services, health delivery and transportation had been maintained or repaired in spite of all the constant destruction. Likewise, the strict Nazi enforcement of police law and order had prevented burglaries and looting.

Now, all these safeguards were gone, as was the propaganda hype of the Reich, and the evil consequences of the war came to light. The times called for endurance and creativity. With the infrastructure broken down completely, the population developed a hunter-gatherer mentality. Burglaries and thefts were common. It was very unsafe.

The gas works had been bombed in Celle, and reconstruction was on hold. Electricity was limited to one short hour a day. It therefore became necessary to provide other forms of fuel. Trees were cut down in the nearby woods, in gardens and public parks, and fences were stolen for home firewood; lacquered street signs burned extra hot. In our garden, the air raid shelter was demolished by the men in our family; Herr Eckhardt helped in exchange for some of the lumber. The support beams were dried, sawed and cut into firewood. A cutting block and saw horses stood in the courtyard, and hatchets, an axe, and various manual saws were carefully guarded. The parallel bars, the tall wooden swing set, the high jump posts, the stilts and the balustrade around Oma's sewing throne all turned to firewood.

Mutti joined the boys when they dug soggy peat in the nearby swamps. This was backbreaking work. Dried-out peat burned well and was needed. Arend and Achim included me in their experiments for making all types of sources of light in the absence of electricity. It is amazing that we did not blow up the place.

Oma's furniture from the turn of the century was comfortable, overstuffed and clumsy. Armchairs and tables were moved around and placed all over the house to meet the most urgent needs of the new house occupants. Bunk beds were constructed and people slept on the floor, in and on anything resembling a mattress, on blankets in window sills, on chairs, on outdoor furniture, and on sofas.

By orders of the British military government, rent could only be collected for spaces that had been leased before the invasion of refugees. But now refugees and displaced persons lived in our bedrooms, closets, attics, hallways and living rooms for which no rent had been collected previously, and could not be collected now.

There was also a strict price control on utilities, which caused frequent friction in the house. With only one meter, occupants had allotments of electricity, but would not stay within their per capita range. The city supplied small sustenance payments for food to new arrivals.

Living in close vicinity with each other did not always run smoothly. Jealousies developed, theft occurred, short tempers flared up, and vengeance came easily. For the Eckhardt and Umnus refugee families, life in the new environment was difficult. Having lost their homes and possessions, having survived a hazardous trek, which frequently brought about the death of loved ones en route, being in poor health, hungry and without means caused many problems.

The locals had their own problems and were not always ready to share. They were tired of hearing stories of escape and loss. All had been better, bigger, easier, more beautiful, and simply more comfortable in the now-gone homeland. Was it? Or was that the creation of wishful thinking? Sarcastic jokes circulated: the dog says to the cat *"They call me a Chihuahua here, but back in East Prussia I was a Rottweiler."*

The house had only two kitchens and two bathrooms, with an additional half bath on the first floor. To manage the needs of all the residents in the house, scheduling became essential. Cooking was done in shifts. The old tile stove had room for several large pots and was in constant use. Wood burning fires needed attention at all times, to be poked, stoked, and rebuilt. Ashes were removed in the morning before a new fire was started. Special iron tools for all these operations hung on a rail around the stove. The ash can stood next to the wood supply box with its slanted top. In the winter, ashes were scattered over snow and ice on the walkways in front of the house to provide traction. Needless to say, melting snow and ashes underfoot were tracked indoors and left a mess for cleaning up.

Keeping the fire burning caused many problems, as all parties had their own wood supplies and guarded against anybody else cooking on "their" fire, unless more wood was exchanged. A built-in deep basin heated water at all times from the exhaust pipe updraft, but whose hot water was it?

With so many families needing food preparation and the utilities severely rationed, cooking time was often early in the morning. If the soup was done by eight in the morning, it was placed into a home built

Kochkiste, or warming crate. This ingenious invention was a box stuffed with hay. Hollowed-out spaces in the stuffing were molded in the shapes of pots and kept the food warm for hours. It seemed that we knew our new neighbors in our old house by the smells of the meager food that was cooked. One family fried a weekly catch of fresh green herrings that reeked through the house for days. Like everyone else in these chaotic times, we settled in.

Garden-grown food was a life saver, as very little other food was available. The garden land had been divided up between the various parties to grow vegetables. Berry bushes and apple trees in the garden were assigned for sharing. Food preparation and preservation was on the women's minds at all times. The bunker lot was now a bean field.

Mutti bicycled to the nearest forest with me on the luggage rack to gather blackberries, blueberries, beech nuts, or mushrooms. This task took a good understanding of weather conditions and growing spots in the woods. In addition, being out alone was very unsafe for women and children, as hungry and homeless strangers were on the desperate look-out for food. Storing food supplies in the kitchen was no longer a good idea, as too many hands could reach for them. Ration cards from the Third Reich were still required for all purchases, but the stores were empty.

People bought permits from farmers for post harvesting in grain fields. Mutti took me along a few times to gather barley, wheat, and rye; we also gleaned pea fields. At home, we sometimes sprouted the grains in water on the window sill and ate them raw, more often they were ground up and cooked into a heavy porridge.

Several times a week our posse of kids from the house, I included, would stand in line at a Herr Matthies' butcher shop, hoping to get our cans filled with greasy water from sausage making. As we waited, an old man would come by regularly, greeting us with "You kids waiting for horse piss?" Nasty jokes were told that reflected the desperate food conditions: "The barber will cut your hair for free. He makes sandwich spread from your greasy hair snippets."

When Oma Clara died in Dissen, her stove was shipped to Celle and put into the one room where our family life took place. Since the central furnace system no longer worked, the house was about to turn into a Siberian ice box in the winter. A stove was a treasured possession, and we were lucky to have our own source for heat and light from the open fire door. Placed immediately next to our regular furniture, the stove was surrounded by sheets of heat absorbing asbestos in the corner of Opa Karl's former office.

Throughout the house, other small coal heaters were installed, as long as they were connected to the old central chimney. A chimney sweep came by regularly for fire safety. We would find his chalk marks on the front door, a ladder and a date, informing us not to light a fire that day. He needed a cold smoke stack for cleaning. Dressed in black, with a black top hat, his sweeping gear slung over his shoulder and riding a bike, the chimney sweep was a sign of good luck.

Our diet consisted mainly of starches. Occasionally Mutti could get horse meat at the slaughter house, no ration cards needed, and we did not know what we ate. Oma would boil potatoes and cover them in a thin béchamel sauce with floating onion slices. Sometimes she fixed a yeast dumpling, big as a child's head. It was tied into a dish towel and steamed over boiling water. We ate it with the stewed fruit that had been preserved the summer before. The dumpling was called *Dicker Michel,* or fat Michael, and was a reference to a pale and rotund 19th century cartoon character in a night cap, satirizing the sleepy German people in their reluctance to get with the swing of modern times and accept democratic politics.

Rutabagas and turnips were our steady fare. Not only during the last months of the war, but even after the collapse. Turnip dominated our diet everywhere, as brightly dyed red marmalade with artificial cherry taste, as fake chocolate cakes, even as fruit drinks. On special occasions, Oma made apple pancakes in her large copper skillet.

Bathing and personal health reverted to almost medieval conditions. The central heating system no longer functioned, and warm water had to be heated on stoves. With only two and a half bathrooms for some fifty residents in the house, standing in line for toilet use was as necessary as the scheduled wash times and bathroom cleaning assignments per family.

Actually, a garden bench was placed in the long hallway near the small half bath to avoid cutting in line while waiting. Frictions developed constantly among the many waiting occupants. The odors of the overused privy mingled with the thick air of heavy cooking smells and fumes from coal stoves, along with the omnipresent cigarette smoke. For the longest time it was my job to fold the skinny local newspaper into small sections and cut them for toilet paper. This job gave me the opportunity to read the paper's juicy installment novel, which I was not supposed to read otherwise.

Laundry days in the wash house were scheduled as well. When the washing was done, we children got a scrubbing in the cooling soapy waters. My hair was washed every three weeks, giving me an itchy scalp in the intervals. The wash house was much in demand by all residents. Like all else, work there was hard and cumbersome. Dirty clothing bubbled and boiled in the tub over a wood fire. That done, the steaming, wet laundry was lifted out, dunked into cold water, and wrung out by hand.

In good weather, laundry posts were installed in sunken holders in the court yard. Cloth lines went up, and the various families had their laundry on display for drying. On several occasions, the tub was scoured extra clean for syrup making from sugar beets. The beets were cleaned, cooked, and squeezed through a press on loan from the neighborhood. The sweet liquid served as sugar substitute.

All this activity made the men in our compound think of Schnapps. Brewing and distilling any kind of alcohol was strictly illegal by British Occupation decree. But it was worth a try to boil and ferment potatoes under Herr Eckhardt's instructions. After all, the lawns and flower beds in the garden had become potato fields, and the spuds were available.

We children were instructed to stand guard and report any spying British military police patrols. In that case, the men would innocently pretend to be helping with the laundry. How thrilling! My father called the resulting brew poisonous *Bärenfang,* a liquid strong enough to catch bears.

Hardly anything was available for purchase, and with nothing to buy, money accumulated. The bartering system and illegal black market activities grew into the only way of maintaining an economy. With the image of hording rodents in mind, city folks went on "hamster" trips to farming communities outside the city.

Another word for these bartering activities was *organisieren.* "To organize" simply meant to obtain items somehow. One could "organize" potatoes, firewood, a cake, a bicycle, and such things. Stories were told about the new fortunes of farmers who had Persian rugs in the cow shed and would trade a sausage for a set of silverware, a dozen eggs for a piece of jewelry. I loved a pair of red suede shoes that Mutti traded from a colorful, bejeweled gypsy woman who wandered into the house although we thought the doors were locked. The shoes were too big. I stuffed them with newspapers until I grew into them.

Another beloved bargain was my set of Dutch skates, again too big and long. They had upward curled tips, and no other child had skates like mine. There was much time for skating on the frozen river in the polar winters of 1945 and 1946. Skates were clamped on to regular shoes and needed to be tightened often, and frequently pulled the heels and soles away from our boots. I often had to take my damaged shoes to the cobbler's shop.

Mutti was delighted when she finally sold one of the large paintings. This picture of a pleasant landscape with a sunlit forest of beech trees had been hard to move. I did not understand the implications of the picture's title. The plaque with the innocent German name for the trees had to be removed from the gilded frame: Buchenwald. Only later did I learn that this title had also been the name of one of the most vicious concentration camps.

My grandmother received a small pension from the filter company. Other than that, no money came in. We lived on the few reserves of saved money.

Cigarettes became the currency of the time. We had no smokers in the family, but we were aware of the cigarette value. Butts in the streets were picked up, taken apart, and rolled into new "coffin nails" on pocket size cigarette makers. British cigarettes from the military had a decidedly sweet smell. The park by the river was littered with butts, as the river had become popular, but not for swimming.

All water sports were strictly forbidden due to the hazards of Polio and Typhoid contamination in the water. But the romantic riverside was now a place for sexual encounters, where soldiers could trade their cigarettes and chocolates for favors. The grass was scattered with slimy condoms. "Don't you touch that stuff. Belongs to the Brits." I remember seeing bloody, oblong strips of cloth by the river. Not knowing anything about sanitary napkins, I wondered why people by the river got hurt, requiring strangely shaped bandages?

The older girls knew all about these things and talked about German women rolling on the ground and in the grass with English servicemen, and they were called "Veronikas." An aura of wickedness and forbidden curiosity hung over these talks in the absence of any information or attempts at sex education. Then it was whispered that our friend Brunhilde's sister was going to have a baby with an English dad, and her mother had figured it all out because the sister had not turned in her monthly bloody rags for the laundry. I had no idea what this talk was all about.

A British medical team rounded up the children by age groups for health screening. I was declared undernourished and sent to a day camp in the forests outside of Celle. After several days of being stuffed with slimy oatmeal, I volunteered to accompany a girl with a twisted arm to the hospital by bus. From there, I walked home and never returned. Mutti's thin soups were just fine, I thought, and the house provided adventure and suspense. There were plenty of kids to play with. Nobody from the camp ever inquired about me, the absentee kid; I could have been murdered or kidnapped.

The potato fields of Celle's sandy soils were infested with hungry potato beetles. By British order, all mobile residents were urged to walk out to the acreages and pick the yellow-and-black striped pests right off the plants. This was a successful community effort; the tubers grew and were harvested in the fall.

The one commodity abundantly available was flag material. For the 12 years of the Hitler Reich, every household had to display the black, white, and red flags with the Nazi emblem in a central circle. Hitler flags were now forbidden, but the material found other uses. We quartered the central Swastika image for cleaning rags.

Like the majority of girls my age, I sported a fashionable *Little Red Riding Hood* look: red skirt, black vest, white blouse. Tailors were much in demand for clothing needs. They knew how to turn army blankets into civilian outfits. They took threadbare, worn-out suits apart, turned the fabric over, and reassembled the garments. Military uniforms were fashioned into women's suits.

The only problem was one of decency: how to hide the give-away stitch marks from a man's fly on a woman's skirt? Women zipped up in the back or on the side, a closure in front was considered most inappropriate, but that strip of fabric could not be wasted. I still wore my brothers' inherited one-piece underwear which had survived the firebombing of Berlin. I learned to adjust the wrong slits in the pants for a girl's pee. My summer sandals were made from pieces of wood nailed together with rubbers straps from old bicycle tires.

School began again for me in the late fall of 1945, in a new location. Since my elementary school house was still a hospital, all four years of grade school children were herded into a smoky beer hall. The place reeked of stale beer, cigars, and urine. We sat on benches at long tables, facing each other, not the teacher. There were no books; all publications were still under censorship by the Allies.

Old Herr Schuhmacher was now the school principal. With cane in hand, on a stage, he directed us to stand up and solve the math problems that he shouted into the room: 97 times 16, divided by 28, plus 315 and the like. The students with the right answer could sit down and kick the other students under the beer tables. Biblical instruction, spelling bees, dictations of ballads that we memorized, folk songs and poetry recitations took up the rest of the day. Recess was in the street; there was no traffic. In the cold months, pupils brought chunks of lumber to heat the place.

Our new classmates were refugee children from all parts of Germany whose dialects we often did not understand. They came from the severely bombed cities in the Rhineland to the west, from the Baltic States Lithuania, Estonia and Latvia in the north, from Pomerania and East Prussia in the east, from Silesia in the southeast, even the sounds of Hamburg to our immediate north were unfamiliar, and then there was a girl from a banana plantation in the former colonies of South East Africa.

We school children participated in a post-harvest potato digging adventure. On that day, my entire fourth grade came to school with our satchels and with garden tools and sacks for the event. I had a shovel. After school, we walked to the nearby whistle stop of a slow country train, rode for a short distance with all our equipment, got off and walked to the assigned fields. The teachers organized us in regular distances from each other in rows, and we could now dig potatoes and keep them. It sounds like punishing work and child abuse or endangerment by modern standards. It would certainly bring protest from Teachers' Unions. But the effort provided welcome food.

Arend, Achim, and their friends Horst and Erich went back to school again as well. Luckily, the three older fellows graduated within a year's time. Achim had to endure more irregular verbs and subjects that did not interest him in the least. I remember an assignment to memorize a very long poem, "The Bell," by the popular 19th century poet Friedrich Schiller.

The poem followed life in town, as the bell rang for

weddings, baptisms, funerals, fire, floods, harvest celebrations, war and victory. I learned it along with him and thought the passages about courtship between the blushing young man and the shy maiden in the meadow were really funny. Somehow this image of a well ordered bourgeois life was out of place!

The traditional school system with emphasis on classical studies must have seemed ridiculously antiquated after the boys' war-time experiences. University study was not possible yet for recent high school graduates as only older war veterans were enrolled. In the meantime, Arend and Achim had no other choice but apply for sought-after three year apprenticeships. Arend eventually apprenticed in a book shop and Achim became an apprentice in an optical firm.

During the summer, there was enough work to be done around the mutilated house until late in the evening. Allied curfew confined us in the house and garden compound, but it was warm and light outside until late. There was no break from the routine: no outside employment, no shopping trips, no travel, a newspaper with local ads only, no radio, no movies, and no soccer games to attend.

When the days were getting shorter and the temperatures colder, strictly enforced curfew regulations pushed us inside. Undeniably, the German population felt anger at the constrictions imposed by our liberators. Neither the German military nor the armament industries drained the country's financial resources any longer, and yet, basic services had not been restored. There seemed to be little difference between the regulations of the Third Reich and those of the Allied occupation.

The space for my family was the unheated former library and Opa Karl's gentleman's small sitting room. With the billiard table gone, book cases now divided the library into several sleeping areas for bunk beds.

Boxes full of china and hastily packed documents and photos or other possessions were piled up under beds and in the corners. All activities took place in the "small room," as we called it. There was the enormous tile stove from Dissen, a red plush sofa from the former salon for Mutti to sleep on, a cabinet, eight chairs, and the dining table for house work, home work, eating, washing dishes, and sewing. Oma, Vati, Mutti, Arend, Achim, Horst, Erich and I, all eight of us, gathered there, but there was nothing to do, and the electricity was off; it was dark.

It was now several months after Armistice. The men had not been wounded physically but had returned to a home that looked nothing like the house of long ago vacation memories. In this bitter winter of 1945 we sat around the dining table in cramped closeness and darkness, eating coarse rye bread with mustard for dinner, alive, not injured, facing boredom. We had warmth and light from the stove, and togetherness. It was cozy in this stuffy room, better to stay there than go to bed in the freezing library-bedroom, where undressing and slipping into the icy sheets required an act of heroism.

The adults had time to think and talk. Was this a time of liberation or defeat? Should we feel relief or mourn the traumas of loss of life, land, and possessions?

Vati had lost his two brothers, cousin Henning was in Russian captivity, and two other cousins had perished on submarines. Germany had started this horrendous war under a power crazed dictator and his followers. We had brought suffering and loss to many other nations. But we had also become victims of our own history. Would we remain under occupation, a divided country, or would we become a responsible Germany again?

Traumatic experiences were touched on, carefully.

There was much to sort through and question, and to attempt dealing with hurting memories. But with the war anxieties behind them, Arend and Achim gradually developed a sense of gallows humor, at least on the surface. It had been ridiculous at times, adventurous, but senseless and absurd.

STORY TELLING AROUND THE DINING TABLE, WINTER 1945

Oma Auguste, the minister's daughter, quoted from the Sermon on the Mount, about the lilies in the fields that did not worry about their clothing, and about the sparrows that found food, and God provided for it all. She intoned Lutheran hymns. *A Mighty Fortress is our God,* four long verses, memory work. *Now Praise We All Our God,* three verses, to be memorized. *The Moon has Risen,* seven verses, by heart. Mutti and I said the last verse of this hymn every night as a prayer for our cousin in the uranium mines of Siberia:

Lie down to rest, you brothers
In God's hands with all others
Cold is the evening air.
From peril do us keep
And grant us peaceful sleep
And hold our neighbors in Your care.

We ended with…And, *lieber Gott,* protect our cousin Henning in Russia.

The Golden Sun Brings Forth Pure Joy, another twelve verses, we knew all the words. This one was my favorite chorale. Each verse described the wonders of nature: the stately rose, the talented nightingale, the humble hen and her chicks, and man, praising the Creator at all times. This hymn had been written during Germany's other, most destructive, thirty year long war some 300 years earlier.

But in our time it was hard to apply these utopian dreams to our conditions. We were not in the mood for much spiritual praise. Many Christmas carols followed. Today I wonder how I felt about my grandmother's insistence on these activities, singing through the darkness in the house. Did I find it odd? What went through the minds of my bothers? But with it she anchored a treasure of strength and poetry in my mind. *Recite the books of the Bible. Know the major and minor prophets. Learn some proverbs in the English language: a stitch in time saves nine; man proposes, God disposes; after dinner rest a while, after supper walk a mile; an apple a day keeps the doctor away.* Story telling was proposed, and so we continued.

Arend talked about his excitement and fear when he was under orders to bring in an enemy pilot from a crash site on one of the small Baltic islands. He rowed there and found the British man in an orchard, happily drunk out of his mind with brandy. The pilot handed Arend his pistol, pointing at himself, and then offered Arend the brandy bottle as well. Arend and some fellow HJ teenage soldiers steered the intoxicated pilot back to their mainland positions.

Vati recounted his train travel to Cottbus, south of Berlin, where a cousin, our uncle Wilhelm Hebbeler owned a textile company and had promised fabric for Mutti and him. Hours on ice cold, windy train platforms, in slow moving, overcrowded trains, no food, no water, cancelled train connections, detours, all a horrendous experience. I suspected that Vati had disguised a geography lesson within this account. The cousin was absent, fighting at the Russian front. His wife Elizabeth and her five children ran the firm while all the former employees were drafted. Vati described how he had given her his textile ration stamps and received beautiful fabric in exchange, but it all burned up in the fires of Berlin.

112

Achim's story of his "vacation" the previous summer was pure adventure, at least at first. He had no vacation at all, but was ordered instead with his classmates to show up in HJ uniform for trench digging to hold off Soviet tanks. The boys received guns and, at 14, were shipped off to Poland. En route, Achim wrote a postcard to Vati and tied a roll of candy to the paper for a weight. He handed the card through the train window to the station master. It had reached its destination! Vati kept the card, saved as a sign of life from his son. Poland had suffered devastating German bombing even before the war, in order to force the population into submission.

Then Achim spoke of staying in the destroyed medieval city of Cracow where they joined hundreds of other *HJ* boys. They were ordered into a grand building, were warned to stay in, but sneaked out through the kitchen windows to explore the city in defiance of their *HJ* leaders. They wondered about the ever-present machine gun installations in windows and on balconies. When their disobedient outing was discovered, they had to turn in their guns as punishment in exchange for digging spades. Relief! Only later did Achim understand that the machine guns were a deadly warning to the Cracow population not to riot in national Polish uprisings as had caused a blood bath just the day before in Warsaw. He also learned that they and the other Hitler Youth troops had been quartered in the former Royal Polish palace. Now, several months after his trip, the German population was made aware of the Nazis' brutalities in Poland. But at the time, Achim did not know that Cracow was very close to the frightening camp sites for people on their way to the crematoria of Auschwitz.

After a few days of back braking digging work at the Dunajec River, Polish partisan sniper fire was reason enough to send the boys elsewhere. On re-entering German lands, they received their "Hitler gift" at the border: a propaganda package with the best food imaginable. The gift was intended for soldiers on furlough to take home and impress their families with the "excellent" military rations. But the boys were still on duty and not scheduled for home. Instead, they gorged on *Leberwurst* (liver sausage) and salami, cheese, honey cakes, chocolate and other luxuries as their train crawled through the High Tatra Mountains. For the hungry flatlanders from the Berlin area, this was like seeing the wonders of the world.

After a day on the train, they arrived at the sandy lands of the Polish North. Here the digging of anti-Soviet bulwarks was quite futile. The trenches caved in, it rained, the boys got sick in their sleeping quarters in the drafty pig sty of a farm, and then they were sent back to Templin. That was the end of his "vacation." School continued as if nothing had happened in the meantime. But these recent stories had lost their adventure appeal and were painful to think through.

On other evenings we boiled the summer syrup down into a thick molasses, or we played games. A home designed Q & A game, Charades, or Pick a Letter, and then find names and words for rivers, cities, composers, writers. S: Sweden, Shakespeare, Stuttgart, Sauerbruch the German physician, Smetana. N: the Nile River, Napoleon, the Netherlands, Naples, Nostradamus. These games might well have been attempts to provide me with a bit of home schooling.

In a different mood, Oma talked about her childhood at the Atlantic coast, where pirate Stortebaker had been a hero, and where sea captains brought back their curious souvenirs from around the world, shrunken heads and mummified creatures and intricate sailing boats inside bottles. One hearsay story was about the Danish war, when a whizzing canon ball sliced off the postmaster's head, just as he was enjoying his morning cup of coffee. I liked her tale of a poor old woman who saved the children in town from drowning. She felt a change in the weather in her bones and set her little house on fire to call all the skating boys and girls away from the thawing ice on the river.

And then there were stories from her adventures and misfortunes in London when she was a young German wife with little command of English. We had heard all those stories before, but were anxious to hear how she would mix up beginning and end of these familiar tales.

Going to the notions store for a few mother-of-pearl buttons was a language story. Auguste had not realized that she was at a wholesaler's. Asked how many buttons she needed, she replied *twelve.* That answer provided her with twelve dozens, a supply to last for the rest of her life. "A dozen dozen," she would say.

She still remembered a little poem about Guy Fawkes, the man who plotted to blow up the British House of Lords a long time ago. Karl and she went to see the bonfires that still flared up on the night of November 5th, she said, to celebrate the failed plot against the King.

Mutti reminisced about her time in Leipzig during the inflation in the 1920s. Money devalued faster than one could spend it. She bought a piece of fish for 500,000 Marks and kept it cold on her window sill, outside. A cat came by and feasted on it, down to the lickety-spit bones. 500,000 Marks! We could identify with a money story. We still used Hitler's Reichsmark with all the embossed swastikas on the bills, along with the simple slips of paper that the British had printed with face value amounts, and foreign looking occupation money, and there was nothing to buy.

Vati had wonderful stories about growing up at the turn of the century in his dreamy rural town of

Dissen. To him and his brothers, Christmas Eve was a test of their patience. With their parents, they attended the evening service in the old St. Moritz church with all the farmers and their families from the region. Right after church, the farmers would come to the Brandt Dry Good store for their Christmas shopping. And of course, Oma Clara had hot coffee and cookies ready and encouraged the ladies to find presents for the men in their families. All the while, Vati and his brothers sat in the stairwell by the closed parlor door, banging their feet and waiting anxiously for the business activities downstairs to be over. What kind of presents would they get? Then, finally, the store was closed and the parlor door opened for the boys to see the *Tannenbaum* in its full glory.

There was one electric street light in town, suspended between the Brandt house and the church. It was great fun for the three boys to turn the light on and switch it off, confusing pedestrians and horses alike. There were stories about the very, very old church: it had been Catholic, then Protestant then Catholic, then Protestant again in the religious wars of long ago.

Vati knew of a curious incident that was recorded in the church registry and was still talked about in town. But nobody had an explanation why the local Baron had had a Black-a-Moore in his employ, or how he had come to Dissen? By town legend, the poor man, or boy, had fallen deadly ill and was baptized on his sick bed. In the presence of several witnesses, he received his new Lutheran name Friedrich Christian. We wondered if christening had made him well?

Then Vati promised to read from an old journal, the next evening, by the light of the open stove door. Early that year, Vati had taken time to dissolve his parents' home in Dissen after their deaths, and he had found several interesting old letters.

"I found this diary in my father's desk," Vati an-

Our great-great-great-grandfather, the music master Johann Philipp Friedrich Kress, Dissen, ca. 1780.

nounced the next evening as he unfolded some old papers. He also showed us a pastel portrait of a friendly old man in a white wig. "This was our ancestor. Just imagine a time some 200 years ago, and listen to the story of my great-grandmother's father, Johann Philipp Friedrich Kress."

It was on the 9th day of November in the year of our Lord 1738 when I saw the light of the world for the first time. My beloved parents were:

My father: Johannes Ulricus Kress who died at the age of 77 in 1775.

My eternally beloved mother: Maria Magdalena Welzerin, who loved me most dearly. Our minister, Herr Esenbeck, baptized me on the 20th of November 1738. My paternal grandfather was Laurentius Kress, a lawyer, wine dealer and barrel maker in Niedernhall; he was born in Nuremberg.

His father, my great-grandfather, was a highly esteemed man about whom I heard many honorable stories in my youth. Not heeding these stories, I have forgotten them all.

"Wait, wait, wait, your great-grandmother's father writes this story about his great-grandfather—how many generations does that make?" Achim interjected. He was the mathematician in the family. "Let's count."

We tried to figure it out on paper.

"1, I, Achim Brandt
2, you, my father
3, your father Franz was my grandfather
4, his father was my great-grandfather
5, his mother was my great-great-grandmother
6, her father, Johann Philipp Friedrich Kress, was my great-great-great grandfather. He wrote this diary, and this is his picture.
7, his father was my great-great-great-great grand father
8, his father, the lawyer Laurentius Kress was my great-great-great-great-great grandfather
9, his father, the highly esteemed man, was my great-great-great-great-great-great-grandfather. That makes nine generations from me to Johann Philipp's highly esteemed old ancestor.

Wow! Go on reading!"

Vati continued:

The above named dear and venerated elders sent me at an early age to the old and benevolent school teacher, Herr Lauterbach. I received instruction in reading, writing, religion, mathematics, music and Latin. My progress was such that our minister, Herr Esenbeck, confirmed me when I turned 13 and admitted me to Holy Communion on Easter Sunday 1752. Immediately upon my confirmation, the congregation voted unanimously to entrust the position of assistant teacher in our crowded school into my care. I also attended to the proper maintenance of the city clock and helped with Sunday ser-

vices. In addition, I became private tutor for the children of Herr Cramer and Herr Kaps.

"My teachers look more like 130 years old, not 13, particularly the Latin teachers," Arend said. We agreed that a unanimous vote for being an assistant teacher with a duty of winding the town clock signaled a serious responsibility. Vati continued:

It was in late May of 1758, on a Sunday. I had climbed the high stairs to the castle for a chat with Miss N.N. who was leaning in the castle window. Just then I saw my good father in the doorway of a pub. He waved at me and bade me come to him. He handed me several letters from my brother Christian in Westphalia, who was a music master and teacher in Spenge near Bielefeld. Christian had already taken a wife and wished nothing more dearly than to see me, his brother, close to him, so that I might fulfill my dreams for further education at the academy in Bielefeld. Full of ardent desire for travel, I asked my good father to allow me to go, and to request of my dear mother to attend to my linens for the travel.

Descriptions of the travel preparations followed. Philipp obtained his passport and assembled a few good traveling companions to join him on the trip. Then there were emotional good-byes from his friends and family, and his father dismissed him at the town gate with many Biblical admonitions. Vati kept on reading about the little group's adventures: how they traveled north, crossed the Rhine River, rested in Frankfurt and continued on their trip for six months, until they finally arrived in Bielefeld and Philipp was united with his brother. He was placed in the academy as a third year student, applied himself diligently to his reading, and received free food in the best houses in town.

"This was right in the middle of the Seven Years War," Arend tossed in. He was the historian in the family, and military history was his specialty. Many countries were involved in this war, but the main enemies were France and England, with the British being allies of Prussia/Germany.

"Just think, if a young man traveled over land, he could so easily be captured by Frederick the Great's headhunters. They fill him with beer until he does not know which way to Bielefeld! How did he travel? On foot, or by coach? Did he have money in his pants pockets? Travelers were snatched by Prussian and English recruiters and forced into armies of ruffians at no pay. The Duke of Hessen sold the young men from his provinces to the British Crown. There they were trained into a fierce mercenary machine and sent to the American colonies to patrol the land."

Vati considered this peril and came up with an answer: "Johann Philipp Friedrich Kress must have been very clever on this journey. Avoiding capture also explains why he crisscrossed around. In Mainz, he was on the left bank of the Rhine River, near French lands, and the French had such a well organized army that they did not recruit strays off the road. He was safe there. And he did not travel alone. The buddies looked out for each other." The image of a beer guzzling ancestor who might get sold and shipped to the colonies on the American continent was interesting, even to me.

"Did the air planes bomb Berlin in that war also?" I asked. No, I was told, this was a land war, and planes had not been invented. But war was war, and no one wanted it. Still, French and Russian and Austrian and

British and Prussian armies all turned on each other, and there had been very bloody battles.

"There have been so many wars in our lands. The troops of other nations have always fought here. The worst was the Thirty Years War, 1618 to 1648. At first the nations fought over their religions—Catholic or Protestant—and then the war turned to land control. Swedish troops owned land in Germany, Spanish troops took Holland, Polish lands fell to the King of Saxony, and there was always loss of life, disease and famine," Vati added.

"But let's see how Philipp is getting along."

More details followed about Philipp's happy time at the academy, where he grew in wisdom and knowledge and perfected his singing in the choir's tenor section, while enjoying his daily free lunches. His good singing voice was detected by the folks in Dissen who needed a music master in church, and, after having paid a fee of 50 gold Thalers to the church dignitaries, he was hired.

Arend noticed that this was pure extortion, shelling out gold to the Arch Dean of the church. Or bribery? Where did Philipp get the money? Had it been concealed somewhere in his coat during the long trip? Was it sewn into his garments? Vati thought that Philipp, being from the South, was considered a foreigner from Nuremberg. Unknown in his new place of work, he might have needed to pay a guaranteeing fee.

Philipp Kress was installed by old pastor Braunes in Dissen who blessed Philipp with these words:

You are the fifth cantor and teacher whom I have installed in my time, and I do not promise you a long life, for, horse labor and hog feed will be your reward!

We thought that Pastor Braunes could have been

a little more encouraging than that at the beginning of our ancestor's career. Hog feed as a reward! One of Philipp's "rewards" was marriage to his predecessor's widow Margarete whose two children he raised like his own. The three children born to the couple passed away soon after their birth, as did their mother. However:

After I had been a widower for a year and a half, a benevolent providence joined me with the young lady Anna Elizabeth Helfers in matrimony on July 23, 1771. She was 19 years old and had been my student. Her father was the respectable master butcher Adolf Helfers in Dissen; her mother was the virtuous Anna Elizabeth Baeckern in Dissen. In this very happy marriage Providence blessed us with the following healthy and beautiful children:

Adolf Friedrich, born 4-3-1773, died 11-25-1773
2) Adolf Philipp Friedrich, born 3-7-1774
3) Maria Catherina Louise, born 9-27-1777
4) Friedrich Wilhelm, born 7-9-1779
5) Margarete Magdalena Friederike, born 4-2-1782
6) Heinrich Wilhelm Theophil, born 7-11-1784
7) Rudolph Friedrich, born 8-2-1787
8) Anna Elizabeth, born 11-9-1788

These living testimonials to our blessed marriage are the noble treasures which the Lord has given us. May the benevolent Father of all Life guide and preserve them and their posterity in Christian prosperity in time and eternity. Amen, Amen.

"Am I your noble treasure?" I was assured of that.

"That was not exactly a rosy life. The job came with an old woman and her children," came from Erich.

"Yes, but remember, Philipp liked clean linen. Old Margarete could do his wash and cook for him," Achim reflected. "And then the guy gets himself a young bride. She was 19 and he was 39. He was 50 when his last kid was born. Where was the school building? Is it still there?"

We had spent much time with our grandparents in Dissen and knew the town quite well. Along with the traditional textile production, Dissen had once seen a flourishing baking trade, and the street names still smelled like gingerbread. When Vati explained that the old school had burned down and a new one was gone by now as well, "across from the church, on the corner of Sugar Brink and Raisin Street," we knew the location. We also knew the old church quite well.

I liked the altar painting of Christ's Ascension into Heaven which is still at the church today. Fluffy pink clouds float across the blue sky above some praying town's people and only Christ's feet are sticking out as He is taken up. Two hundred years earlier, Philipp had looked at the same picture that we saw. If I could meet Philipp today, I would ask him about his musical contemporaries. J. S. Bach and G. F. Handel were of the same period; Joseph Haydn and the Mozart family had become popular musicians and composers. Had Philipp ever heard of them? Did he know their music? Would he have liked to be a court composer or was country life preferable? Did Philipp compose his own music to play on the organ in church? Did he write it down, or did he improvise as he played? Did he have much time for his music, or was he consumed by teaching obligations and *horse labor and hog feed?*

"The teachers lived in the school house," Vati added. "Philipp's youngest daughter Anna married her fa-

St. Moritz Church in Dissen.

ther's young colleague, Matthias Brandt and that is our name to this day. He came from a long line of teachers and music masters, and they lived in the school house with their children as well.

"That must have been crowded like we live in this house now! Old Philipp Kress with his Anna, their daughter Anna with her husband Mathias Brandt and their children, and then holding school in the same building! Think of the noise!" was Mutti's comment. Vati thought that the many deaths in Philipp's family might have been caused by Tuberculosis, deep in the walls of the school house's living quarters.

"The teachers were not paid, they had to collect their income from the students' parents," Vati added.

"Was that fair?" Arend asked. "That makes teachers just like any workmen, like carpenters or shoe makers. But Philipp had gone to the academy and learned Latin and such stuff. What did he teach in his school?"

Vati provided more recollections from the old sto-

124

ries that the town's people used to tell. "The teachers taught reading and spelling. All the children had to memorize Psalms and Bible quotes. They probably did not have enough desks for all students to sit and write, at least not at the same time. And, math was taught for an extra charge!"

"Can you imagine how much time it took every day to remind the children and their parents to pay? And to collect and record the fees? There goes half the lesson time," said Arend. "I bet the farmers didn't much want to part with their money. If I had three children, I would rotate them and pay for only one!"

Vati continued reading, and we had gotten used to the elaborate style of the 18th century language:

For long, I thought, the sun of good fortune would smile on me, but an increasing weakness showed that the Angel of Death had entered silently. Fate tore my unforgettable wife from my side, after we had lived richly blessed and hand in hand for thirty-five years. She died the first of June, 1805, and her once so active and now lifeless body was placed into the quietness of the grave on the fourth of the month.

Philipp even included a long poem:

Words of Consolation
End, oh end, come to me soon
Wipe my tears in the new moon
End the yoke that binds the slain
End the rule of fear and pain
End the mighty worry stone
Make it change to gold alone.

End, oh end, we pick the rose
Israel's desert life will close

End, oh end, my hiking cane
Takes me home where I am sane.
End, oh end, my fear and fright
Turns the harvest to delight.

End, oh end, in Canaan's land
Israel's freedom is at hand.
End oh end, Mount Tabor 's near
Just beyond Mount Olive's fear
Jacob then is homeward bound
Where no Esau will be found.

End, oh end, such lovely word
Sweetens all of pain's sharp sword
When the rock is hit by force
See the Godly balm spring forth.
Ah, my heart, take note of this,
In the end we meet in bliss.

Arend wanted to know how long Philipp lived after his wife's death. Vati knew the date: 1820.

"Then he lived right through all the reforms under Napoleon."

"Yes, correct."

Vati explained that Napoleon, the French general, had crowned himself Emperor in 1804, conquering much of Europe, Germany included, and French became the main language. Napoleon also brought many good changes that modernized the country. He ordered a reform of the legal system, education for all children, simplification of the currency, and limited the influence of the Catholic and Protestant churches. England was Napoleon's main enemy, being in an alliance with Russia, Sweden, and Germany. Napoleon blocked all sea trade from the continent with England. When he invaded Russia, his troops perished in the swamps and icy winter of 1813.

"Sounds just like Hitler's Russian offensive" came from Horst.

Thinking about Napoleon's church reforms in Germany, Vati remembered that, according to family stories, even the music masters in Dissen fell under these new regulations. They could no longer supplement their meager income with fees collected for singing at weddings and funerals. As for Philipp, he was an old man, with a strong, traditional faith, which he expressed piously in this diary.

On another evening sitting around the table, Oma Auguste said that she knew of an old diary from about the same time, when Napoleon's French administration had created a great deal of confusion in her native Schleswig Holstein. The diary was from her family. Would Trude look for papers in the second drawer under the bookcase by the window, in the library-bedroom?

Further instruction followed and indeed, a ledger was found with business entries from 1812-1823. The author was Auguste's grand uncle Karl Heinrich Spethmann from the Hamburg area who managed a leased farming estate. In addition, he was a trader, dealing with buying and selling of wheat, rye, oats, barley, wood, live stock, or any other commodity. Mutti thought we would get a feel for the difficult situations at his time—war, foreign soldiers, no money, confusing currencies, and a bank reform on orders from Napoleon. Actually, Oma's native area of Hamburg had been part of the French Empire, and there was no love lost. Troops from other nations all around, and the Russians were friends this time. She picked some of the many entries and started to read:

Monday, January 4, 1813: *Saw Herr Gattges from Lübeck who told me that the French army had marched on Russia with 500,000* to 600,000 troops, and all but 50,000 men were alive now. Even these few men were surrounded by the Russian army, and that Russian soldiers had entered our German town Königsberg. He also showed me two white mice which came from Russia and were very cute.

Thursday, January 7, 1813: Herr Kroll came over to buy 50 tons of rye for 4 Thalers, but I wanted 14 Louis d'Or and would not sell under price. This was risky for me. My lease money is due today, and I lack 450 Thalers. I will wait and see if they take me to court or extend my credit. I have no doubt grain prices will increase.

Friday, January 8, 1813: Kroll came back and bought the 50 tons of rye at 14 L which he will pay in silver on Monday. I did well, waiting it out.

Sunday, January 10, 1813: I rode over to Oldenburg for church and heard that wheat sells for 17 L, barley for 9 L, and oats for 6 L. I am glad I did not sell my grain yesterday.

Sunday, January 17, 1813: The decree about the new Reichs Bank money was read in church today. We can only hope that this regulation will be to our advantage, more so than the old paper money which will become invalid on February 1.

Monday, January 18, 1813: I went to Brockkrüger this morning where I talked to two men who came from the trade fair in Kiel. They said that the introduction of the new money had caused turmoil, and nobody liked the change. The Hamburg bankers withdrew all their deposits and cleared their accounts. The sale of several aristo-

cratic estates was canceled because there were no buyers.

Friday, January 29, 1813: *Went to the lumber auction in Sebenter, but prices were too high for me. I bought three loads of scrap wood at 3 Thalers. After the auction I dined with head forester Mr. Vogel and head inspector Mr. Meier and heard that the French Emperor Napoleon may be dead.*

"Well, on that he was really wrong. Napoleon was not dead by a long shot," came from Arend.

Saturday, January 30, 1813: *I crossed over the frozen lake this morning to get to the mill in Farve. This was my third time to call on the miller, Mr. Engel, but he is never home to pay the 49 Marks for the grain I sold him. I really need the money. I have a loan of 3 Thalers and 36 Shillings from Broeckkrüger, and Demoiselle Petersen loaned me 1 Thaler and 32 Shillings. My bill for lumber is due. I can collect outstanding income from sales in Heiligenhafen, but payment cannot be made for 3 weeks. I have more than 100 Thalers in paper, but they will be worthless on February 1.*

Wednesday, February 3, 1813: *Today is the third day of levying recruits for the regiments in Oldenburg. The Commissioner of War was here and visited his sister, Demoiselle Petersen. Last night, I became the happy father of a healthy boy.*

Tuesday, July 27, 1813: *I heard a rumor that English troops have occupied southern Denmark and have blockaded the Baltic. Supposedly 1,000 French troops are still in*

Lübeck, but the Danish quarter master is already requisitioning beds for 7,000 Danish sharp shooters there.

I was totally confused. Our ancestor had debts in Thalers and Shillings, and sold his goods for Louis d' Or and Marks, and there were coins and paper bills, and all of it sounded like a colossal computing problem. "Were there Danish armies and Russian soldiers, and English troops in Germany? And French soldiers too? That would be so frightening. I would not know where to run!"

I was told that all these armies tried to drive the French back into France and capture Napoleon, the French Emperor. Figuring out the different currencies was a headache. Languages were a problem, and there were never enough supplies. The towns' people always wanted to make some quick money from the foreign soldiers, and the soldiers were looking for loot and girl friends.

Wednesday, July 28, 1813: It is rumored that Armistice between the warring armies will be extended to August 15. Driver David Hengs from Preetz was en route to Hamburg with a load of butter. Supposedly he turned around and brought his butter back to safety. He worried that the French would stop him, take his butter and require that he drive for them.

Monday, September 6, 1813: We all went to Johannisthal for harvest beer where we enjoyed the company of 42 persons in all.

Saturday, September 11, 1813: We had harvest beer at Wesseck. Except for those that did not show, there were 32 persons and 18 horses. Herr Bading's band from Oldenburg played harvest beer music. He was paid 2 Thalers and 24 Shillings.

***Tuesday, November 9, 1813:** It is rumored that the French lost a big battle near Leipzig on October 18 and 19. The Allies stormed Leipzig and captured the King of Saxony. Napoleon Bonaparte supposedly escaped from Leipzig just an hour before everything was lost. I heard that the French lost 30.000 men on the battle field, and another 30,000 troops were taken prisoners. The Allies captured 800 carts with gun powder, a large number of canons, and 200,000 guns which the French had hidden in Leipzig. The French Emperor may have offered peace negotiations. My hired man Peter Libker rode over to the estate at F. and heard that all their men are with the auxiliary corps, and all but two are seriously ill or injured. One man from the corps wrote to his wife that he will be home soon, but she should not be frightened because he left one hand on the battle field.*

All the adults discussed the famous Battle of Nations at Leipzig, in our country in 1813. The victory over Napoleon had been a cause for great celebration and pride in Germany, but the country was impoverished and suffered for many years from the great losses of life in that war. I wondered who had done all the counting of men and canons and gunpowder. What happened to all the prisoners of war? Did they have camps for them, and hospitals? We certainly heard much about POWs and returning veterans in our recent war. The adults around the table did not really know. More reading:

Monday, November 29, 1813: I obtained two machines for flax threshing from Dittmann in Nessendorf. In three and a half hours time, we made four and a half pounds of flax from 21 pounds of straw with eight flax workers at the machine. The machines cost me 16 Shilling each. I believe I can do better in the traditional flax threshing methods with women doing the hard work by hand.

Mutti pointed out how threshing used to be done with heavy threshing poles, a very demanding job for women, while the men sat back and counted their profits. She was getting tired of all the war entries. Information continued about Swedish, Russian and English troops in the country through 1814 and 1815. The financial situation did not improve for our diary writer. Cows and pigs sold under price. She finished with one last entry:

Saturday, January 28, 1815: I was invited by Herr Kropp to join the festivities for our King's birthday. But I do not have enough money to go and will stay home. I also did not want to spoil Liese's entertainment. She counted on going to the dance because she can present herself as a marriageable candidate at such occasions. I was going to drive Liese and Mademoiselle Ehlers to Oldenburg, but then the administrator from Farve and his secretary, Herr Daniels, Herr Engel, the miller, and the administrator of the Lange estate all came by here to see the ladies, whom I trusted into the gentlemen's care. The road is snowed under, and they must take passage by way of Seekamp, through the pastures and over the frozen lake, along Poggenhoff, and over the new dike.

We all agreed that the demoiselles had an exciting ride to the dance, and we hoped that Liese found her heart throb.

All these events around her native region brought other memories back to Auguste. She told us that her grandfather had been a tobacco importer in Hamburg. Inspecting his bales of leaves one day, he discovered a colonial worker who had fallen into the tobacco during shipping and was pressed into the bundle. He was dead, but preserved, shriveled, tanned brown, and a mystery.

"I wonder what they did with him?" Achim asked. "That takes a lot of explaining to the harbor master. Do you think they buried him in the city cemetery? I bet he was a heathen!" "No, they threw him in the Elbe River with bricks in his pockets" was another suggestion. It was a curious case for speculation.

Steeped in thoughts about her family, Oma remembered the broken and repaired China plate in the dining room. She wanted to show us the plate and tell its story. But her dining room was now occupied by the Blanke family, and she would have to go next door in her own house, knock on the door of strangers, and ask for her plate back.

That done, and once again around the table at night, we looked at the plate from close up. The plate was glazed in raised decorations of flowers and leaves in soft green and pink hues on the front and underside. Oma turned the plate over and produced an old envelope with a slip of paper that was tucked into the iron clamp around the beautiful plate. She read:

*The mother of my great-grandmother was **Mrs. Von der Wettering** from Holland. She lived in Wandsbeck near Hamburg and gave her oldest daughter a set of China dish-*

es for a wedding present. This plate is the only remaining piece of that set. Supposedly her husband was a sea captain and brought the set back from China.

*Her daughter, **Maria Wettering** married **Herr Studt**. She was the third wife of her husband. The other wives had been her sisters and died childless. She gave the plate to her oldest daughter*

***Maria Studt Lützo**, born 1797, died 1857. She gave the plate to her daughter*

***Maria Luise Lützo Spethmann**, born 1818, died 1878. She gave the plate to her daughter*

***Agnes Spethman Baetz**, born 1842.*

That is about all I know about this plate. I want the plate to go to the oldest daughter in each generation whose name begins with an A. Please do not laugh about the family history on a plate.

Agnes Spethman Baetz

Oma folded the paper and returned it to the envelope. "This note was written by my mother, **Agnes Spethman Baetz**. She died in 1925. The plate has come to me, **Auguste Baetz Hebbeler**, and it will go to your Aunt **Annie Hebbeler Ohlendorf**, and then to her daughter, your cousin **Almut Ohlendorf**. Perhaps there will be many more girls who will inherit this plate. Almut will always be welcome in my house, and so is her brother when he comes home from Russian captivity."

Almut had finished her studies in Microbiology just before war's end and was a freshly baked PhD, living far from the Hamburg area, and far from Celle. We were sure Almut would find a husband and have a daughter: Amanda, Anneliese, Alma, Anastasia, Annemarie, Agatha, or something like that. Today,

Almut's daughter **Annette** has the plate, and her daughter **Alina** will someday receive it. Alina lives in Wandsbeck near Hamburg, where the plate originated; she is the tenth generation holding on to this heirloom.

Back at the table for evening readings, Vati produced a package of letters from his maternal grandparents that he had found when he dissolved the household in Dissen. These letters took us back again by almost a hundred years and yet they had a familiar tone. Both grandparents had written to the grandmother's brother, who was enlisted in the War against Denmark in 1864. The grandfather cheered the soldier up:

> *Aplerbeck, March 6, 1864*
> *It is good that you are off duty from the front lines. We hear that you had plenty of action recently. But in spite of all the discomfort, you probably have a lot of fun with the war. Whenever that many guys are quartered together, some fellows will make the others crack up in laughter. Just put your gun powder and bayonets to good use and win soon. We look forward to your return and think that you will be promoted to Corporal. Then you will proudly march home from the field of honor and display your well deserved medals.*
> *Greetings, your brother-in-law.*

To this the grandmother had added:

> *Good to know that you are well, just keep warm in the rough winds. Little Alma talks a lot about you "Uncle Carl in war in Slewi Holsten." We hope that you show those Danes their place and come home soon. Then you*

can eat Easter eggs with us.
Your loving sister Jette

We ate our main meal at lunch time, *Mittagessen.* Not a day without the blessing:

Come, Lord Jesus, be our guest
We thank for food that You have blessed.

Cabbage soup, rutabagas and steamed puddings that filled us like balloons. Only flour, yeast, water and a bit of sugar were needed for this dish. On special occasions, a glass of our canned cherries was opened for the pudding. In the evenings, it was a slice of bread with mustard and herbal tea, peppermint or chamomile leaves that we had gathered in the summer and dried.

Friends once sent us an ammunition crate full of turnips. But in the Siberian climate of the post war winter, the shipment arrived frozen and spoiled. We were not sorry. Turnips and rutabagas were still the main food staple. Rutabaga flour for rutabaga cake, turnip mousse with artificial chocolate taste, turnip tea had been the fare, enough to not want to eat.

Among his father's papers in Dissen, Vati had found his paternal grandfather Friedrich Wilhelm Brandt's passport and journeyman's book with the official stamps from his travels, 1842-43. The grandfather was the only son among his eight siblings who did not immigrate to America. He had apprenticed as a tanner and dyer of textiles. Dissen had long been the center of linen weaving in every cottage, but machine industries were beginning to threaten the local manufacturers. It was customary that young men traveled around the country for a year or two after their apprenticeship was completed. They worked with master craftsmen in other cities in order to perfect their skills.

The small book was passed around the dining table. It contained only the seals of cities that he had visited. Occasionally he stayed longer and worked for a master textile dyer. We wondered how he had traveled. Had he taken trains or boats, or was it all done on foot? Wasn't there a pretty girl somewhere so that he returned to that town? No, he traveled east, west, north, south. The comments from police officers and city commissioners attested to his good behavior and clean appearance. The last entry stated that he had entered Switzerland illegally and without the proper authorization. Therefore, he was ordered to return to his home town without delay. We assumed that he found his pretty girl there, because, otherwise, we would not be here reading his journals.

All brothers and sisters of Vati's father and paternal grandfather had immigrated to America in search of a more prosperous life.

Friends of Adolph Brandt (with top hat, like Abraham Lincoln) honoring him at a beer party on his return visit from Chicago to Dissen, 1890.

Several of these ancestors had come back for a few return visits. One of them had become a music professor in Springfield, Illinois, and another uncle had a good position in the flourishing beer industry.

Our grandfather in Dissen had saved a letter from 1892, inviting the family to come to the Columbia World's Fair in Chicago, where pumpernickel, sausages and German beer were most popular.

Another letter from our grandfather's American brother Adolph Brandt spoke of the dilemma in World War I, when the United States and Germany were enemies. Adolph had lost his work and income with the Busch Bavarian Beer Company due to Prohibition. The letter was dated **Chicago, July 18, 1919**:

My dear brother Franz,

Finally, after many years, we received permission from President Wilson to write to our loved ones in enemy lands. I waited for three days to collect myself for this task. It weighs on our hearts to find out what became of the family. How are you, your sons, and their friends? Have they returned from the war, are they hurt or disfigured? I wait with fear and worry for your answer. May God watch over your life. Let me warn you: I am not sure what we may say in our correspondence; we must be careful.

Newspapers here reported about the Russian terror when the Czar was still in power. But here, in the so-called land of the free, we have been dictated laws that put Russia to shame. Whoever was of German descent found himself in a frightful situation. But all who were born over there and immigrated here, were even worse off; they were and remain "Huns." It has been very difficult for us Germans here. We were shunned as spies, even if our sons fought with the military overseas.

A report followed about all the family members who had been in Europe with the armed forces. They had returned safely.

Letters were opened and censored or stolen. If a person mentioned the slightest criticism he was told to leave and go home to Germany. Thousands and thousands were sent to various camps as prisoners, even if they were American citizens. Many are still incarcerated today.

It cannot be denied that there were many war profiteers. Not me! I have lost <u>everything.</u> And that after having worked in this country for 51 years. I am as poor as a church mouse. Fanatic groups play a very important role here. As of July 1, all pubs have been closed. Wine, beer, or whiskey cannot be served any longer. Congress declared January 20, 1920 as the day of Prohibition. The president ordered that, in case the war was not over by July 1, 1919, no more liquor!

Well, in Chicago the war is not over. The city has 7,500 restaurants and beer gardens that bring in $1,000 each in license fees and taxes. I am one of those thousands of employees who lost their jobs in the distilling industry. I would never have thought that the American people take all of this without protest. Before the war, we Germans were on the side of the liberals, but today, we must keep silent.

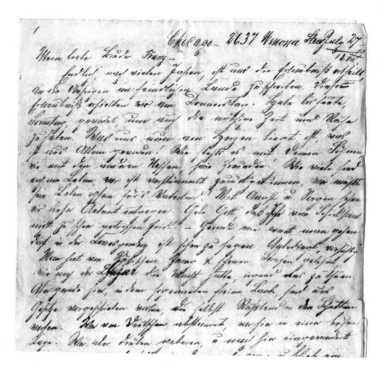

Letter from Adolph Brandt, Chicago, 1919.

The letter continued with more information about increasing prices and worries about the future. However, our relative and a few German business partners had decided to start a *Whole Sale World Wide Importing Company.* Ironically, the relatives in Dissen were to ship Westphalian hams, bacon and sausages, which would hopefully be in high demand in Chicago.

Around our table, we had much to discuss about this letter. Vati doubted that the importing business ever came about–and would German imports have been popular in that anti-German climate? It was inflation time in Germany, and no one had money that was worth anything in the 1920s. He reflected on the bitter lot of German immigrants who had been welcome a few years prior, and were now detested.

We could not imagine life without beer or wine, it was part of our German identity. And no funds to live

140

on. Even in our sparse times, we had some subsistence payments from city or government sources. American relatives had always been seen as the lucky ones who lived in the land of milk and honey, but this was a different story. Mutti spoke of the moral stress for young men in World War I fighting in a country where cousins might tragically stand on either side of the firing line. We wondered how the family had fared in the years since 1920.

The younger generation of these American relatives whom we did not know found our address and sent care packages. I remember cans of corn and barbecued beans. Corn was never eaten in the German diet; this was a new food, and so were the spicy beans. Included in the gift were balls of crocheting yarn and a pair of delicate, ruffled gloves in pink nylon for me. To my embarrassment I had no idea where and when and how to wear them, and they did not match my persona in the Little Red Riding Hood dress from flag material.

Vati figured out that the kind sender was a distant cousin from the Chicago area. We thought that their packages brought us odd gifts, but the considerations were appreciated. In the following years, Vati would compose letters to the relatives, which Mutti translated and I helped with my school English. More recently, I have tried to verify the information about German spy camps in World War I. Since I could not find much information, I wondered if stories about these camps had circulated as victimization myths among the German immigrant groups. But there is some vague evidence that the camps did exist.

In the late fall, Mutti decided to dig Karl's coin collection up before the ground could freeze and the moisture would corrode the metal. Dug into the ground under the carefully stacked logs in the wood shed, the package could only be retrieved at night, and she would have to do it by herself, because the help of others would look suspicious. Actually, all collections needed to be registered with the British Military Government and would most likely be confiscated. As my brother tells me, we registered Grandfather Karl's collection as permanently lost in the East, now under Soviet occupation. But even before digging it back out, the question was where to put the coins? Karl's safe in the paneled dining room was now the place where the lawyer Blanke family lived. Could Vati initiate a considerate discussion of the situation, relying on the legal training they both had?

Mutti went to work at night and started digging as if on a treasure hunt. But then she was interrupted by one of the curious refugees from the house. She had to quickly cover her digging efforts up, shift logs around and pretend to get a load of fire wood. When the coast was clear, she dug the box out again and piled the logs back in place on top of the freshly turned soil, all in one long night. In the mean time, the two jurists had come to an agreement. They decided to trust each other and store the items back in the old safe in all secrecy. They probably handled this somewhat illegal issue with traditional formality, addressing each other as

"Herr Doctor" and "Herr Doctor."

The very cold Christmas of 1945 was approaching. Mutti prepared the traditional dough for crispy cookies, using the syrup we had pressed earlier in the year. With water, flour, syrup, and pepper, cinnamon, nutmeg and other spices these cookies were cheap to make, crispy, and absolutely delicious. She had also made arrangements with a baker in town for the use of his large baking hall for a fee. This was a lot of fun: early one morning, but after the baker and his apprentices had already baked their breads and hard rolls, and when the ovens were still hot, we could do our family baking there. We wrapped the dough in towels, packed our cookie cutters, and pulled the load to the bakery on our cart. Then we were permitted to use the large tables and rolling pins in the bakery. We cut the goodies in our favorite shapes and placed them on baking sheets that were wider than my arms could reach across. Into the ovens and wait! It was warm there and so much to see! Letting the cookies cool took willpower, but they needed to be sampled and were found tasty beyond words. Oma's rather large metal hat box from England was our cookie jar.

Achim had somehow obtained all the supplies for a jig saw project. With a sawing block clamped to the oak dining table, the two of us went to work on making all the figures for a nativity scene. I learned how to hold the saw straight up, not angled, to be careful not to break the blade, and how to turn the plywood while I sawed along the penciled outlines for my characters. We made Mary and Joseph, the Christ child in the manger, the shepherds, angels, kings, a lantern, an ox and a donkey, and a flock of sheep and a dog. We sandpapered our creations. We cut and glued small blocks behind the figures to make them stand up. For paint we only had a watercolor set from school. The pigment soaked right into the wood, requiring re-

Hand-made jigsaw nativity scene from 1946,
still used in the Brandt family, 2013.

peated coats of paint. We were really, really proud of our achievement and used the scene for years under the Christmas tree. Achim still has the whole group, now painted and varnished in shiny acrylic coats.

Arend and I discovered another nativity scene. This one was in the shop window of butcher Matthies, and we looked at it in admiration. Sausages and a ham on display would have been stolen out of the window. But this arrangement was safe from thieving hands—it was sculpted in tallow. While our nativity people were flat, these figures were fully round, three dimensional, all made from grayish white fat, and looking like marble. The baby was there, Mary and Joseph, the angels, the shepherds with their lambs, and the kings. I was taken by Mary's curly hair and the cute wooly sheep. In his irreverent sense of humor, Arend explained that Mrs. Matthies had probably put a chunk of tallow in her mouth and pressed it through a gap between her teeth, and out came curlicues!

British soldiers treated the children of Celle to a Christmas party in a vacant movie theater. Entertainment films did not play yet, they were still under the information control policy. We arrived with trepidation among so many uniformed men. But we were ushered into a bright hall, all decorated with unfamiliar green holly and British flags. Friendly soldiers greeted us and showed us to our seats. It smelled of Lysol and cleanliness. We were asked to stand for *God Save the King*, and then we saw a fairy tale production, put on stage by men of the occupying force in drag costumes. They spoke English, but we knew the story. *Silent Night* was intoned on the movie organ, and we sang along. Santa came with bulging stockings for each of us. Inside, we found unknown wonders with foreign tastes and smells: Cadbury chocolates, oranges, chocolate chip cookies, peanut brittle and striped peppermint candy. This was certainly the way to win the youngsters of Germany to a new life after the war!

In school, too, we received hot meals that had been prepared in a British military kitchen. Every child went to school with a tin can on a wire handle and a spoon. We stood in line in the school yard at recess and waited for the teachers to scoop our fare from large canteens. The food was predictably one of three soups: pea soup with floating, swollen crackers, bean soup with corned beef, or lumpy milk soup with oatmeal. One of our teachers had returned from Rommel's African campaign where he had been taken prisoner in a British POW camp. He told many adventure stories about his survival in the desert sands of Tunesia. He had also experienced the thrill of getting plum pudding in his Christmas rations as a prisoner. Now that we were getting canned plum pudding in school, he created an atmosphere of total suspense before tasting it. He pushed his Swiss army knife into the tin can, rotated it carefully and pried the lid off, smelled the pudding's spicy fragrance, let us know that it smelled irresistible, and scooped out a bit with his knife to taste. So good! Then he went around from pupil to pupil with pudding on the knife tip, and we all licked it off carefully and a little scared of the sharp edge, feeling like grown up survivalists.

My friend Ilse was very excited at this time before Christmas. Her mother had talked to a returning soldier who had seen her husband, Ilse's father, in a Prisoner of War camp. Networks like this were established and helped bring displaced family members back together. Now Ilse's father would come home for the holidays. Her mother bought a tree and decorated it with candles and apples and gold glitter. In loving anticipation they talked about the man that Ilse hardly knew. The tree was so pretty. Life was promising in the cozy warmth of their kitchen with the fresh, fragrant pine. When the tree began to dry out, it was moved to the freezing bedroom where it would stay fresh for some time longer. But by Easter the barren tree was tossed out and Ilse's father did not return. Like so many of my friends, Ilse was raised by a single mother. Absent fathers were treated with respect; they had become heroes, having given their lives for the country.

Ilse lived with her mother and grandmother in a small apartment behind a storefront that had once been the family's grocery shop. An enterprising refugee had turned the tiny space into a barber shop and beauty salon. Men and women customers sat right next to each other. The barber had fashioned an ingenious construction from the old toilet system for his water supply. With the toilet removed, the water in the old tank high up on the wall was now heated by an electric coil, whenever electricity was available. It was a very slow procedure. A lucky customer would get a hair rinse with warm water that ran from the tank through a hose to the one sink in the shop. The tank had formerly been operated with a pull chain to deliver flushing water for the stool. Indeed, necessity was the mother of invention.

I remember little about celebrating Christmas in our crowded room. We ate those wonderful crispy cookies. Arend had done some volunteer work at the museum and surprised us all by showing up as Santa, in a bright red 18th century British uniform on loan from the museum's display cases.

With the New Year approaching in 1946, the house and its occupants changed again. One of the two lawyer families eventually moved out, but new occupants were in line. A physician with his family lived upstairs from us, and the sharing of kitchen and bathrooms continued. Herr Eckhardt, the carpenter from the garden pavilion was now joined by his wife and several children, and they all moved into some of the recently vacated rooms in the house. He and his girlfriend came to a friendly agreement as she now shared her one room with her parents and daughter. The pavilion now had an electric line stretched from the main house and dangling above the terraced garden. An oven was installed with a venting pipe out the window, water had to be carried in, and an outhouse stool existed in the freezing cold tool storage under the house.

My brothers' two friends each located family members and moved out: Erich had found his grandfather in another town, and Horst joined his sister, the only survivor of his family. Shortly after their departure, a cousin, Ute moved in with us; she attended the local poultry research institute and was a wonderful helper in our attempts to raise chickens for eggs and the soup pot.

Unsorted, one-day old chickens were cheap. We purchased several and placed them in a box in the bedroom. Heated bricks between pillows and blankets served as mother hen. Our efforts worked out and the cute fluff balls grew into various chickens—Leghorns, Rhode Island Reds, speckled red and white hens and a few mean roosters. When it turned warmer outside the rather stinky mess moved into a poultry yard and shed that was constructed around the former *Kaffeklatsch* grotto. Nobody had time or coffee to enjoy outside, and the chickens liked the stone perch. The hens grew and began to lay eggs which Achim recorded in a farmers' almanac. The birds became a valuable food source for us. One night a hungry fox sneaked into town and found our improvised chicken farm. He grabbed one of the girls and ran from the screeching screams of her frightened sisters. The birds needed better protection. A shelf system in a storage closet by the kitchen would serve as sleeping place. We corralled the chickens every evening, grabbed them under their wings, and brought them in. The reverse process happened every morning before school. Chickens are messy birds and their nesting place in the house needed to be scrubbed clean regularly. And all before latex gloves were on the market!

Slowly, jobs became available. Vati would do some archival work here and there. After high school graduation, Arend offered his English language skills as a tour guide for British officers in the local museum. Generally, the officers had much free time on their hands. They were well educated academics who were familiar with German history and philosophy and took an interest in this land of their former Kings. Arend invited two officers who had expressed an interest in looking at Opa Karl's English library. They visited a few times, sat around the table with us and talked. When they brought oranges, we realized that we had never seen this fruit before. I received a gift of a Brothers Grimm fairy tale book in English, which I could not read, but kept for many years. To Mutti's intense shock, one of them had flown in the devastating bombing missions over her beloved Dresden.

The German population was hungry for programs that would reach beyond the daily struggle and comfort the mind after all the shallow fare, disinformation and propaganda of the Nazi Regime. Museum visits became popular. The choir began to rehearse again, and I was accepted into the Bach youth choir. To this day, the mystery and magic of choral compositions goes straight to my heart. Then, we sang under the watchful eyes of a British officer. Sheet music was inspected for censored print materials. When communication was finally established with the officer, he turned out to be a minister of music himself, eager to hear the music of Bach in the German language.

Mutti suggested a scrap book project of collecting art pictures. Calendars and magazines, when available again, printed photos of art works and architectural sites that had been destroyed or lost to the East, or had survived the bombings. This effort reminded the population that great works had existed in our culture and that German artists of the past had traveled and created their works just like artists in our neighboring countries on the European continent. Not all things German related to extermination and war. I loved the project and learned to distinguish architectural styles of town halls and churches and castles by their period. At ten or eleven years of age, I saw myself as an expert on Gothic cathedrals, Renaissance sculpture and palaces, and romantic and modern paintings as I filed my grainy newspaper pictures into their right time slots. I loved it, and it gave me something to do.

But more than anything else, manual labor was needed in the beginning reconstruction of our devastated country.

Herr Eckhardt, the carpenter, found work in the castle. Queen Caroline Mathilda's wing was to be restored for future public access. There were broken windows and crumbling walls in rooms that had been empty for a very long time. Along with all the remodeling, it was time to build and paint display cases. The population in Celle would soon learn that the castle had become a collection point for art treasures from the world famous Berlin museums, and exhibits would soon open.

Although much older, Berlin was laid out as a modern city with broad avenues in the early 19th century, "Museum Island" in the city center came about, surrounded by canals and rivers. It was conceived as an impressive show place with several elaborate buildings for the Royal and Imperial collections of paintings, sculpture, and more art treasures. As in other Royal Houses, collecting art demonstrated the importance and power of the monarch. The collections had grown to include priceless archaeological marvels and artifacts from around the world, all of which were threatened by air raids in the war. Already in 1941, the holdings had been removed from the museums to subway tunnels in Berlin. With the near total destruction of the city, these locations were no longer safe towards the end of the war. In early 1945, ten convoys of hastily crated artworks evacuated from Berlin for storage in empty mine shafts, underground, in undisclosed locations. These transports to the West had the same objective as the migrations of refugees who were pouring in: survival and escape from the advancing Soviet Army.

When the war was over, and under US leadership, the Western Allies actively sought to find these locations and retrieve what had been stored and what had been looted from other countries. These efforts were empowered by the Commission for the Protection and Salvage of Artistic and Historic Monuments (Roberts Commission, the Monuments Men). General Patton's Third Army liberated the salt mines of Merkers and Grasleben, not too far from Celle, where gold, some 400 paintings and antiquities were hidden. Collection points were established in the American Zone to record, photograph, study, and preserve these finds. Eventually, storage locations in the British Zone became part of this retrieval effort as well. The castle in Celle was chosen as one of the destinations to care for and display the rediscovered collections from the

Kaiser Friedrich Museum in Berlin. I do not know if looted objects were among the treasures that arrived in Celle.

When the show rooms finally opened for the display of art, the public was treated to rare exhibits. Chinese scrolls, ancient Greek pottery, German romantic paintings, Polynesian masks, Egyptian sarcophagus portraits and other rare collection pieces appeared in changing exhibits. Professional curators were appointed for the care of these art works. They had no idea what the unidentified crates might contain and were surprised about discovering unexpected treasures. Due to cramped storage and adverse climate conditions, some artifacts needed to be cleaned and professionally restored. I remember a display of "before and after" paintings, showing damage from inappropriate handling, and restoration. An incredible richness of artistic and archaeological works could be studied in our small town. The exhibits answered the needs to see and admire beautiful objects for a culture-starved population. In this intimate environment where the castle windows overlooked familiar streets and shops, the exhibits had none of the stagnant formality famous museums used to have. I have since rediscovered and visited

My photo of a scroll from an exhibit of Chinese art in Celle Castle. I had scribbled "Chinese lady killer" on the back.

some of the familiar objects from my youth after they returned to Berlin.

A newcomer in my fifth grade had moved into the castle with her family. As romantic as it sounded, their living quarters might have been right for by-gone times, but they were ice cold and lacked all amenities except for a pretty view from the castle tower windows. She was the daughter of one of the art historians assigned to the restoration project. We became good friends and explored the old building and cold passageways many times.

In addition to his work for the display cases for art, Herr Eckhardt also worked in the scene shop of the small Baroque theater in the castle. In an effort to reacquaint the culture starved population with serious drama, a troop of actors began to perform once the immediate needs of the city had been settled. Mutti subscribed to season tickets, and we saw a wide variety of classical and modern plays by German and international authors over the years. Sometimes we speculated about the set decorations. With a limited budget, sets would reappear on stage with some form of carpentry alterations. But we had not anticipated what we recognized in an Ibsen play: there were our grandmother's sofa and arm chairs from the Eckhardts' rooms in our house! True, the turn-of-the-century pieces were appropriate for the play, and he had probably charged a fee for loaning them out.

MORE STORY TELLING

We still spent our evenings around the family table, no longer under curfew, but still with hardly any electricity. The winter of 1946-47 was approaching, and the situation in town was getting worse. By now, the few resources stored from earlier times had been eaten up, people were getting weaker and restless, and the winter set in with muscular strength. The population felt victimized—Germans had been the perpetrators in the war, but now, two years later, we were still under very similar restrictions to those of the Third Reich, imposed by the British occupation. A change was due.

For us, the readings continued around the dining table. Mutti read 19th century ballads. Vati chose to tackle Homer's *Odyssey,* book by book, and adventure after adventure. Here was a long poem of mystery and ghosts, of monsters and love, of dangers, betrayal and loyalty, of gods and goddesses. The ancient poetic meters fit the German translation just fine, as if we spoke in hexameters ourselves. Princess Nausicaa from a friendly island palace was my favorite. I could picture her with her girlfriends bathing by the olive grove and attending to their laundry—just when Odysseus, a tired, nude man was washed ashore! All the episodes and characters invited explorations of my imagination. Only years later did I realize that Vati had carefully selected this ancient text as it described the hero's struggle to stay alive, often in the face of death, on his long journey home after the Trojan War. But he did get home to Ithaka and found his family alive. The real stories of life never change.

There were also some letters from Vati's maternal grandfather who had traveled to a health spa hoping to cure his lung ailments. His detailed descriptions illustrated the medical treatments of the time quite well. He wrote about his trips to Frankfurt and to the Rhine valley. These letters sounded amusing to us. During her husband's absence, Vati's grandmother Henriette ran the little family bank in town and reported regularly about payments and expenditures, along with good admonitions for her husband's health. Germany had become an Empire by the time the letters were written in 1875, and the currency had changed from older denominations to Reichsmark. Accordingly, great-grandmother's letters from her banking business recorded the confusions over the old silver pennies, Reichsthalers, Florines, French Louis d'Ors, and the new Reichsmark. The bills from the spa were still included with the bundle of letters and listed expenses in all these currencies. This currency mess was very similar to the financial problems that our Hamburg trader had recorded in his diary fifty years earlier.

August 11, 1875

After arriving, I rested for a little while. I checked out the list of guests in town, and found the name of my old friend Marx from Herdecke. I dressed in a hurry and went to see him, but was told that he had gone to Frankfurt. Me, off and gone to the spa park, where a band was playing most beautifully. I sat down under a tree and watched the people from all over the world in their colossal finery and different get-ups. Then I mingled in with the people at the tables: and there was my friend Marx! He was overjoyed, and we talked till late at night.

M. picked me up this morning at six o'clock. We went to the bath house for our curative drinking waters, and I downed quite a few glasses. A crowd of people had already gathered, all walking around in the strangest morning robes and with their glasses in hand. At eight we went to Dr. Brocking. His waiting room was full of patients, but M. gave his card to the nurse and asked if the doctor could see me right away, which was granted. The doctor examined me thoroughly, like no doctor ever before, and prescribed two glasses from spring number 3 every morning. I must not eat anything greasy and should drink a half bottle of light red wine every evening with carbonated water.

August 14, 1875

I am quite happy with my condition. I am not coughing as much, and the sputum is gone. I don't cough in the mornings, but at night when I am lying down. My body is somewhat out of order from all the water drinking, from perspiration, and diarrhea. My appetite is so-so, and I am tired, but that is the rule with newcomers in the first week. We eat in a restaurant with about one hundred other persons. It is pretty good. They serve: fresh, lean soup with barley, beef roast with potatoes, followed by white cabbage with pancakes and ham, then dishes full of stewed plums with mutton roast, then a good pudding, followed by fruit.

We thought that this much food would make us ill rather than well. Pancakes with cabbage sounded particularly objectionable. Vati read on:

This is how I spend my days: up at 7:30, walking till 9, breakfast, then I write letters or read, walking in the spa park at 12 for an hour, then I eat lunch till 2:30 and sit in my room till 4, then I walk in the forest with a friend from here. At 6 we both drink our milk. Many farms here are ready to sell right after milking. The spa guests crowd around the barns by that time, young and old, rich and poor, and we drink the milk warm, right fresh from the cows. The milk is very rich and costs 1 ½ silver pennies per liter. I drink my fill and walk till 8, and then I have dinner. I ordered 3 eggs for tonight, but I am not very hungry. The doctor allowed me to smoke and drink beer, but I don't have the taste for it. I go to bed at 9 on the dot. With this routine, I am bound to get well.

August 20, 1875
Dearest Henriette,
I am feeling fairly well, but I cannot get better in this dreadfully hot weather. It is easy to catch a cold, in spite of all precautions. The thick linen shirts that you packed for me are pure torture, I could not stand them. One day I did not wear my undershirt, which the doctor had said not ever to do. Then I put on my under jacket and wore a pleated shirt. With these changes in my wardrobe I caught a cold. Would you please send me two lighter shirts and another pleated shirt? The sun burned my skin and I look like a mousey-fur guy. My love to you and our dearest children.

Vati's grandfather's lung ailment was probably

Tuberculosis. He passed away after a second stay for treatment. The letters were written in the most positive tones and made his terminal treatment sound like an adventure, but we could hear the distress.

The colorful descriptions of medical treatments and living conditions motivated Achim to offer these letters to the Historical Archives in Soden, which is still a popular health spa today. The documents were most welcome, as the city was planning an exhibit of the area's curative mineral springs, and no information existed about doctors, housing, restaurants and cultural activities. However, patients' lists were on record, indicating that the spa had been particularly liked by guests from Czarist Russia. The writer Ivan Turgenev had stayed there in 1860, Peter Tschaikowski was listed as "a nobleman from Moscow," not as a composer, and Leo Tolstoi enjoyed his stay so much that he included a Soden beer garden scene in his novel *Anna Karenina.*

It seemed that the cold winter would not end. The younger members of the various families in the house still spent many hours after school skating on the frozen river. We were home in the evenings, still a family of seven, trying to stay warm in the small room. We sat around the table, Oma unraveled Afghan blankets to knit the wool into scratchy garments, I had a sewing assignment for needlework class in school, and the others shelled walnuts from the tree in the garden, talked, and read. When the electricity was rationed, we opened the fire door of the stove and had light.

Grandmother Auguste surprised us all with a few letters that she had saved from her late daughter Edith, our mother, when she had been a newly-wed in far away Pomerania. Vati did not know of these letters, and was visibly moved to hear Edith's voice speak from these pages. Mutti Trude and he had become good partners, but at times he was still grieving for his Edith. "Here is a letter from your trip to Danzig (Gdansk) through the Polish Corridor in 1926," Oma said. "You can tell she did not like the Polish-German complications." The Polish Corridor had been cut into German lands after World War I and had been the reason for Hitler's invasion of Poland at the beginning of the Second World War.

Lauenburg, June 1, 1926
Dear Mother,
Our trip to Danzig was terrible. The train was very full and so hot I almost died. We were locked into the compartments and wanted to open a window. Right away a Polish soldier came and yelled at us, we understood that we were not supposed to open the window. At the border, the passport inspection took a long time on the German side, but even longer on the Polish side. Then we crossed into the Polish Corridor. Polish military was everywhere and all signs have been changed to Polish names. You cannot imagine how filthy the train stations looked. Otherwise, the trip was beautiful, traveling along the Baltic coast. The Poles built a very large port in Gdingen. We saw three torpedo boats. In Zoppot we arrived on German soil again, but we were still not permitted out. Then there was another short curve through Polish land, and we finally got back on German soil in Marienburg, where the doors were unlocked. The entrance to the town is breathtaking, seeing the ancient castle with all the ramparts and fortifications.

"Here is another letter, a week later"

Lauenburg, June 10, 1926

Dear Mother,

I am pleased to tell you that I survived my big laundry day, and I am proud of it. The entire house took a real interest in this wash fest, and everyone was willing to loan me their tools and equipment, because I don't yet have all the necessary things. The laundry woman came with an exceedingly blessed appetite and brought her 13 year old son, who just happened to show up for every meal with an equally good appetite. I leased the laundry drying lot from Herr Abrahams and put up my clothes line there. Well, my initiation was a downpour! After that I had the best of luck, and all my pieces were dry by noon the next day. We quickly folded all the sheets and table linens and towels and sent them to the mangle after lunch. That done, I had about an hour's time to go to the Women's Association fair. Was that ever a cheery happening! So much going on! It started to rain again, and we all got stuck there. We stayed together and ate piles of sandwiches. The chairwoman was a good organizer, tall, stately, dressed in black, leaning on a cane, just the image of a lady aristocrat from Upper Pomerania!

There were other letters from our mother reporting about her daily life, so far away in time and place. She proudly talked about the furniture that her parents in Celle had given the young couple as a wedding present. I had no recollection of my mother; she had died when I was a little girl. But I remembered the dark mahogany furniture that had moved with the family from the Polish border to Berlin and had gone up in flames there. These letters established odd connections in me to the mother I had not known, but who spoke to me about her life, and I felt a sense of humor from these old pages.

Reading and talking continued. The 50th birthday of a very close family friend was approaching. What to give him as a present? Since there was nothing to buy, creativity was the answer. Vati was still in the mood of reading ancient Greek hexameters. He decided to write a classical poem that would be ridiculously out of place and over the top in its elevated tone, and we could all help. So we sat and counted syllables and meters to get it just right. The idea was that a big celebration in uncle Otto's honor was to go on, with each of us wishing him the best that we could imagine. Food was abundant and wine flowed in this fantasy scene. Each of the eight verses described one of us, sending him wonderful foods that bespoke the hunger of the time. The poem ended with this wish:

"Auguste, the ruler of family fortunes and household affairs
Raised up her glass and commenced in the following words from her heart:
"Dearest friend Otto, may health and fortune and good food aplenty
Friendship and love surround you in honored retirement pace.
Sacred goddess of old, Peace, may you come Stay with us all, and remain as never before in our land.
Bring him some liver pate from Paris, and lobster from Maine,
Bring him sweet cherries and apples, honey, pork chops and beer,
Bake him a cake with eggs and fresh butter, with chocolate and nuts.

160

*Family bonds shall be strong, and wine shall
always be flowing.
Thinking of times yet to come, this winter of
forty and six."*

In our small room, the evenings of talking and
reading had now lasted through the second winter.
When the weather turned warmer, Mutti had a surprising announcement:

"Remember the suit cases that Vati carried out of
Berlin and left behind in the cloisters of Hamersleben?"
she asked one night. "I am going to get them." Vati was
quite opposed. The cases were in what was now the Soviet Zone, and getting across the border from the West
into the East was very dangerous and illegal. Guards
were stationed in shooting distance from each other. How did she think she could get past them? Then,
even if she did get into the Russian Zone, how would
she get out of Soviet control? Would she be able to locate the suit cases? Would they still be with the friends
where Vati left them? Would they have been plundered
empty? Then what next? Hitchhike around, a single
woman with two heavy suit cases? How would she get
back from there into the West? But Mutti had figured
it all out.

"I am going with a woman who has crossed over several times before. She goes to the border section that
runs across fields, and she knows a guard that she can
bribe. I trust her. I have to be ready to crawl through
the field when he is on duty." She was determined and
could not be dissuaded. All further arrangements and
bribe payments needed to be made right away. We all
realized that the only way of getting out of the Russian Zone was by detouring through the Russian sector of Berlin. A divided city, Berlin was surrounded on
all sides by Soviet territory, but it was possible to get
from East Germany into East Berlin and cross from

the East sector to the West sector in the city, and then leave from West Berlin. She had studied the maps and knew where to go. Mutti took the train to the departure point. We did not hear from her for a week, and then she was back, but without the suit cases that had been the reason for her daring trip.

This was her story: it had been a very cold and frightening night when she found herself in a group of three other border crossers. They waited in a field until the signal came to hunker down, duck, and run across the green border. Once across and out of firing

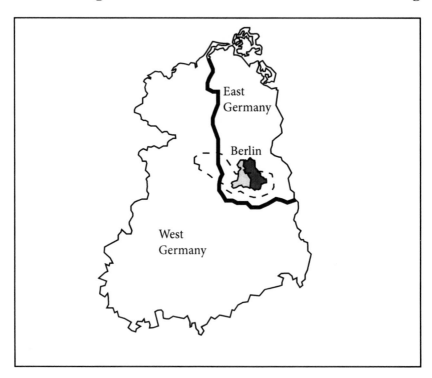

Mutti's illegal trip through East Germany.

range, they stayed in a farm house and cleaned up, no words were said. From there she bought a train pass with the old Reichsmark currency and traveled to Vati's friends, who, indeed, were still in their house and had the suitcases. Next was her trip to East Berlin with the baggage, another border crossing into West Berlin, and there she expedited the suit cases at the train station for shipment to Celle. This would take a while, as freight trains had no schedules and would be delayed as they traveled through the Russian Zone, then pass inspections at the border between East and West Germany, and travel on to Celle. She herself had endured the same return trip on a slow passenger train, and there she was.

"You made it across five borders!" Achim said. "Into

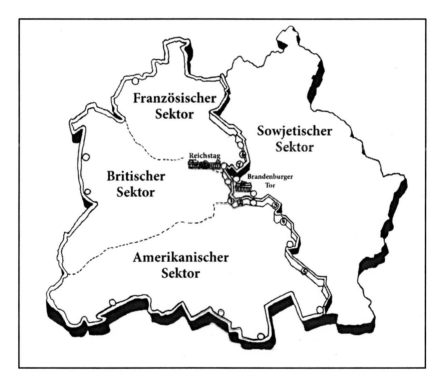

Divided Berlin inside East Germany before the Fall of the Wall in 1989. The western part of the city was jointly administered by the French, British, and American Allies.

East Germany, into East Berlin, into West Berlin, into East Germany, into West Germany. Our compliments!"

Post World War II Germany was divided into east

and west sectors, and had become a much smaller country with one quarter of her land lost to Poland and Russia. Mutti's trip through Soviet controlled East Germany took her into divided Berlin which was surrounded on all sides by East Germany. With Unification, the division of Berlin and of the country ended. The Federal Republic of Germany's eastern border is the former Iron Curtain.

The well traveled suit cases eventually arrived. If Mutti had waited, the trip would not have been possible. The uneasy conditions in Berlin, the capital city, had gained in intensity. Communication with East Germany was becoming near impossible, and crossings between the two parts of Berlin would eventually be stopped by the Wall, which was built by the Communist East. All of these tensions were leading to the Cold War. The armistice treaty had left Berlin a divided city surrounded by East German lands under the rotating administration of the Americans, the British, the French, and the Soviets. When the Russians escalated hostilities against the West Berlin population and cut off all land access, the Western Allies came to the rescue and dropped water, food, medical supplies, and even a power station into the old Olympic stadium of the West Berlin sector.

Herr Kohlmeier, the father of the family across the court yard, in the old servants' quarters, was now a truck driver for the British army. His regular assignment routes included deliveries at a near-by British military air base. Herr Kohlmeier took Achim and me once to the outer perimeter of that air field, and we watched supply planes taking off for Berlin every three minutes. Grateful West Berliners called the planes "our chocolate bombers." This effort came to be known as the Berlin Air Lift. It saved the city from starvation and disease.

I am not sure what Mutti brought back in those cases.

Mutti Edith's hand-embroidered table cloth, 1930.

Some of the sterling forks and spoons I inherited may have come with her. I know for certain that one item from this adventure has followed me all the way to the United States. It is a round Christmas table cloth that Mutti Edith had embroidered before I was born. She stitched angels, Christmas trees, Santas, donkeys, churches, and fat geese—the traditional meal for the Christmas feast—in cheerful, bright yarn. The yellow goose is as big as the church, and Santa is even taller than the steeple. It is amazing how one piece of cloth can carry so much history and meaning.

That same spring, and still in our limited space, a surprise letter arrived and provided new speculations. It came from a relative of Uncle Wilhelm Hebbeler, the fabric merchant whose family Vati had visited not long ago in Cottbus. We did not know this relative, but he wanted to come and discuss certain issues with us. Could he stay overnight? Well, such an undertaking required careful shuffling about in our crowded ac-

165

commodations. He came, Uncle Roderich Rembrandt Fiedler. He was a painter and sported a flowing red beard. I wondered to myself whether he placed his beard over or under his comforter at night? It seemed like an important consideration. Roderich Rembrandt came to tell us the tragic story of the family in Cottbus.

Coming home from the Russian front, Uncle Wilhelm found his country villa occupied by a guest of the Third Reich. His house in town had been bombed to the ground. His wife and oldest three sons had perished in the raid, while the younger two sons were still alive. The Russian army was advancing on his town, the war was lost. In despair, our uncle Wilhelm shot his two sons, and then turned the gun on himself. This had happened in April of 1945, and it was now more than a year later. It was well known that the Russians confiscated all properties of absentee owners, this one included. We, as the closest relatives, needed to establish an inventory of lost possessions in the East, Roderich Rembrandt told us. Actually, there were several houses in addition to the country villa and his residence, the factory and other business properties. And then followed the most astonishing tale about the Grand Mufti of Jerusalem.

Several years earlier, the country villa in Cottbus had been seized by the Nazis and given to a friend of the Hitler Regime from Palestine, the Grand Mufti Haj Amin al-Husseini. This Palestinian nationalist had been president of the Supreme Muslim Council in Jerusalem. As an outspoken Anti-Semite, he had incited many riots against the Jewish population in Palestine, which was a British mandate at the time. The British authorities wanted this trouble maker out of the country and encouraged the Mufti's trips to Germany. Since Husseini had already established friendly relations with the Nazis, and supported Hitler's war and extermination policies, he was welcome in Berlin.

The Nazis confiscated Uncle Wilhelm's villa for Hitler's friend Haj Amin al-Husseini, the Grand Mufti of Jerusalem.

In order to keep the Palestinian guest away from bombing danger, the Party confiscated the country house of Uncle Wilhelm, and moved him there. When we heard the story it was not known whether he was still there or had returned to Palestine after the collapse of Germany. What to do next?

The whole story seemed too absurd to believe. But Husseini is indeed a historical figure, and pictures show him with Hitler. This friend of the Nazi regime was no longer welcome in Germany after the war. He returned to Palestine and continued to be an antisemitic agitator.

Roderich Rembrandt Fiedler accepted all responsibilities for further enquiries. Somehow, his visit was characteristic of the difficulties of communication and the scarcity of information. All media, newspapers, journals and radio broadcasts were under the censorship of the Information Control Office of the Military Government. Mail was slow. A personal visit was the best way to discuss these sensitive events.

In a similar manner, we lacked news from other relatives and friends. Had they survived the war, and what had become of relatives now in the Russian Zone? The cadets on the submarines had not survived. Aunt Annie's son, we had heard, was a prisoner of war in Russia, working in a Uranium mine, and would not come home for five years. The friend in Stalingrad perished like thousands of other soldiers, but Mutti's friend from the Africa Corps had written from a camp in the Arabian Desert near Cairo.

As to the visit of Uncle Roderich Rembrandt Fiedler, the enquiry into the property ownership started a process that is still not settled, almost seventy years after our first discussions. This story reflects the checkered history of post war Germany with the rising antagonism between the Western Allies (the United States, Great Britain, and France) and the eastern part under Soviet control. Since the property in Cottbus was in the Soviet Zone, or German Democratic Republic by a later name, the West established compensatory payments for lost properties. I received a small payment with accumulated interest in 1968. With the fall of the Communist system in 1989 and Unification of the two German states, the property became available to the original owners again, but re-payment of the earlier compensation was made mandatory. Arend, Achim and I all paid the sum back, and we are waiting for the sale of Uncle Wilhelm's land. With German thoroughness, the heirs to the various parcels of land have been found across the globe. While my brothers and I are relatively high on the list of heirs, one relative can look forward to an eventual compensation of $1/2048^{th}$. The amount of sheer book keeping is sadly comical.

NEW PROSPECTS

After completing fourth grade, I was admitted to the week-long entrance examination for secondary school. German High School started in fifth grade and continued for nine years of stiff pre-academic instruction. High school reflected Germany's efforts to hold on to a challenged class system. My play friends Ilse, Marlies, Ursel, Bruni and Inge all went to Middle School for another five grades and from there into apprenticeships. Our paths had separated. My school was the same Empress Augusta Victoria School for Girls that Aunt Annie, Mutti Trude and Mutti Edith had attended; co-education had not arrived yet. As a fifth grader, my hours were in the afternoon and early evening, as the building was occupied by other students in the morning. Lack of built space was everywhere! I walked the two miles each way through town and through the castle park for the next nine years.

Our teachers were returning veterans and refugees. Building an existence in the post-war environment of a new place was as difficult for them as it was for many students. The story telling from our winters around the dining table continued in school, and we were cautiously curious about the teachers' backgrounds. Our Biology teacher had sustained a serious head injury which left him with a distorted face and his jaw bone partially blown off. We knew how many dresses our teachers had—no more than two. Our Math teacher started to wear a ring which made us giggling girls tease the lonely man about a fiancée? He finally told us that the ring had been made from splinters in his spine. I loved our teacher for English and German, Miss Hinz. She was a refugee from far-away East Prussia, and she often talked about the beauty of the lost land. We read the *Diary of Ann Frank* with her. It had just been published and had particular relevance for us with the close vicinity of Belsen, the camp where she had died. We read modern poetry in Miss Hinz' class and wrote query letters to the poets, even collecting money to buy a fountain pen for our favorite writer. Miss Hinz started a correspondence with friends from student days in London, at a time when such international connections were still difficult to achieve. As tenth graders under Miss Hinz, we raised funds for a trip abroad, got our passports, and participated in an exchange program with a British girls' school. In London, I discovered the old address of my grandparents and found Karl's name on a plaque in a neighborhood church.

I found a copy of Eugen Kogon's book *Der NS Staat* in the bookcase at home and was so shocked at the horrors of the Nazi Regime and the experiments with human life that I felt the need to read in secret, and in shame. What I read was too inhuman to talk about, but I remember including my thoughts in the long essay discussions that we had to write in school. *No Exit,* by Sartre, printed like a newspaper on grainy paper, was another early response to the recent experiences. Our history lessons in school ended with a study of the 19th century. Teachers lacked the critical distance to tackle more recent events; poetry, prose and the visual arts expressed the spirit of the times more fully, and more experientially.

Vati received a stirring reminder of the recent past when he searched for information about his brother Hermann's death by German bombings in Holland. "Friendly Fire" is a vicious euphemism for having been killed by one's own side. Vati shared the moving letter from his Dutch friend from grammar school days. The friends had corresponded during student years and in early married life—my father in his legal profession, and his friend as a theologian, but then their letters had stopped. Wem Zydner lived in Rotterdam, a city that had suffered devastating German bombardment. In 1946, with the war over for more than a year, Vati approached his old friend, hoping to hear if his brother's name could be located in a military cemetery. He received the requested information from his old friend, along with news of personal losses and the destruction of his home and church in the 1940 bombing of Rotterdam. At a time when so many people had lost their faith in a just and merciful God, pastor Zydner's faith had been strengthened in the hope for a better future:

Rotterdam, Sept. 28, 1946
Dear Wilhelm,
Your letter brought back many memories. I am delighted that you and your children are still alive. You write that we must spend much time, talking. That is so hard for us when we think that our German friends covered up the cruelties of the National Socialists, even if there was no choice. I met Pastor Niemoeller at a conference. With him, all bitterness fell from me, and I knew that I was speaking with a brother in Christ...

After the war, I was elected president of the General Synod of the Dutch Reformed Church. I travel abroad in this capacity; perhaps I will be in Germany and can see you.

I am not writing this to find a good ending for my letter when I say that the only way to save the world is in the hands of Jesus Christ.

I experienced this truth when I saw the evil people committed on each other. Only through Him was it possible for me to love my enemies.
   With best greetings,
   Wem Zydner.

Christianity's roots in the Jewish faith presented problems in a Dictatorship that practiced extreme antisemitism. In this, the Nazis continued the beliefs of an earlier extreme right wing Lutheran group that sought to toss out religious teachings related to the Old Testament. Trying to retain a semblance of traditional Christian beliefs, the Third Reich created the "German Christians," preaching a doctrine by which Jesus had been born to a Germanic soldier father, thus making Christ an Aryan of Nordic ancestry. Pastor Martin Niemoeller was an outspoken opponent of this assault on religion. As one of the founders of the Confessing Church and a tireless critic of the nazification of churches, he spent seven years in concentration camps but survived execution.

Vati traveled with his brother's daughters Helga and Erika to their father's burial site in the Netherlands. The two friends Wilhelm and Wem met at that time. They had carried heavy emotional burdens which they overcame as they renewed their old friendship. The two countries also repaired their neighborly relations.

Today, the long road to coexistence within the European Union has achieved a fragile climate of cooperation, providing the longest time of peace the continent has ever experienced. Personally, I was excited when one of my graduate students sent reports about his studies in Political Science at the University of Cracow. The bombed-out city where Achim had been as a teenage draftee is now charmingly restored, and Poland has become a member state of the European Union.

POSTLUDE

It took almost ten years for my grandmother's house to return to normalcy. The oak paneled dining room and the solarium were ours again, and the potato fields became flower beds. Life was slowly getting better. Elections were held as early as 1946. A confusing number of parties were founded after the Nazi's one party rule was over. The conservative Christian Democrats would be predominant for many years, but there were also the Social Democrats, the Free Democrats, the Communists, the German Party, the National German Party, and many smaller groups representing expelled refugees and evacuees by their region of origin. Germany was still under the military administration of the four victorious Allies; therefore, the Communist Party was still on the ballot, and anti-American sentiments were not uncommon. Left wing groups had painted *AMI GO HOME* on our garden fence. Vati saw the unintended irony by which *ami* meant *friend* in French.

By 1949, Germany was experiencing an economic miracle after the currency reform and the introduction of the Deutsch Mark which brought full employment. The Federal Republic of Germany (West) was founded, based on the Basic Law, (the Constitution) which provided for the eventual reunification at some time in the future. Reconstruction, housing developments and the automotive industry began to boom in our densely populated country. The Western Allies had succeeded in promoting democratic ideas and an appetite for a competitive market economy.

But the vestiges of limited space were still there, in Oma's up-side–down-house: up to the end of her life, Auguste slept in her former salon, with book cases setting off a private bedroom for the old lady of the grand villa.

I still visit my family and friends in a land that has changed into a very different country from what it was in my youth. I look at the Germany of today with a certain degree of nostalgia, with admiration, and shock. I understand the country's history, but I bring an international perception that questions the challenges of our times in both countries. There is also the question of my own identity. Is it one of German background, or has my identity been formed by my adopted country? I had two mothers; how did each of them shape me? A question of nature versus nurture?

When the family letters were read around the dining table during those two winters after World War II, there was nothing else to do. Our evenings served as debriefing sessions for recent experiences. Some of these readings sound downright nerdy today. Perhaps it was the very personal nature of these old correspondences that drew our attention. Perhaps a sense of pride spoke from the letters. They reinforced that families had existed and cared long before us in their own times of war. They certainly gave us a feeling of continuity and confidence in those horrendous upheavals. The letter writers of old had been able to face their perils and joys, and so could we, in anticipation of new beginnings. Anecdotes filled the "long ago" of linear history with real people and events. The letters and conversations also opened a wide world to me, quite beyond our narrow living room at the time.

I recognize the realities of long ago as not that different from today. Worry about money, illness and war has always been with us, but the force of life overcomes turmoil and hatred. I cannot recall much complaining; there was plenty of reason for it, but to what advantage? Our day-to-day activities focused on immediate needs, without radio entertainment or newspaper information. We talked, and the family grew close.

The English word for HISTORY takes its meaning from a Greek root implying a fabric, as if woven into a textile pattern, or into a living organism. The German word is GESCHICHTE, and the word relates to layering, like the tasty treat of a *Schichttorte,* a layer cake. Both these words are rich in associations. When I ask: "what is my history? What is my story?" I can feel the threads and layers of stories from former generations. Does my love of music go back to the old music master? Does my love of travel come from Karl's trips with his filter equipment? Do I have a sense of what I am willing to pay because of the commodity trader's calculations on rye and lumber? I am very fond of hand crafted things. Does that interest come from Mutti Edith's textile skills? I admired Vati for his sense of fairness and integrity under troubled circumstances. Mutti's interests certainly influenced me. She was a woman shaped by the contradictory experiences of the time, a bright, sensitive, tough, courageous, and very caring aunt who became our mother. I am grateful to know that this fabric exists in the family.

Grandmother Auguste's faith was undeniable and carried her through disastrous times. She deserved absolute respect in her black dresses, we almost feared her; we would not cross her. She did not have the greatest sense of humor, but she knew who she was, and she expected us to know the same. Auguste certainly saw herself and her house as a safe anchor in those disturbed years.

A few days after Christmas one year, Auguste

gave me money to buy replacements for the burnt-out sparkler ornaments in our tree. This mental image is as paradoxical as the times were: my austere grandmother wanting to watch dynamite sparks shoot through the dry branches of our live Christmas tree.

The historical perspectives taught me to appreciate ironies and contradictions that surrounded us, but I also developed a sense of distrust in political leadership. It was not a very rational world, but rather a lesson about odd human experiences, stretching from pure evil to generosity. The heart and brain are so resilient that a painful past can become just a memory. I do not feel that the Nazi ideology left an imprint on me. The Nazis preached the creation of a new, racially pure nation. But achieving a new man, a new society can be found in other political systems, in Communist and Fascist thinking as well, and American Presidents have set such goals. The upheavals of the time were felt in our family and in the house and garden, and in the community and city as well. Our garden had come full circle—it had given us pleasure and recreation, shelter, a hidden storage place, food, fuel, and provided enjoyment once again. Our city had changed from a romanticized Royal Residence to a town with a malicious past, to overcrowded town conditions with endless shortages, and now Celle sparkles as a popular, colorful tourist destination. In all of it, Celle has struggled to incorporate pride, blemish and progress.

My history, my story is the fabric of all my stories and experiences. And I know that, as an immigrant, I have carried memories of those lives with me into my new home. I am lucky to have all these references. I think all immigrants bring such gifts.

Shoemakers' Lane in Celle, December 2013.

EXPLANATIONS

My memoir deals with the events of World War II and family life in the post-war period under Allied Occupation in the British Zone. Frequent reference is made to earlier times in Germany's complex history. The following explanations may help to orient the reader.

1st Empire, "The Holy Roman Empire of the German Nation" (800-1804)

Thirty Years War (1618-1648) hymns p111, church in Dissen p116, 121

Seven Years War (1756-1763) Philipp's diary p120

Napoleonic Wars (1804-1813), the commodity trader's diary p127

Danish War (1864) letters to the front p135

2nd Empire, Kaiserreich (1870-1918), Herr von Schluter p28, letters from a health spa p154

World War I (1914-1918) Vati p15, letter from Chicago p135

Weimar Republic (1919-1933), Polish Corridor p115, 158, Inflation p115

3rd Empire, Drittes Reich (1933-1945) Nazi Period

Allied Occupation in American, British, French, Soviet Zones (1945-1949) Divided Germany, Cold War, Mutti's illegal trip p162, Uncle Wilhelm's tragic story p166

Federal Republic of Germany; German Democratic Republic (1949-1990), Fall of the Wall (1989)

Unification, Federal Republic of Germany (1990)

GERMAN PRONUNCION

Achim	A-kim
Arend	Ah-rent
Celle	Tselleh
Christiane	Kris-ti-ah-neh
Mutti	Moo-teeh
Vati	Fah-teeh

ABBREVIATIONS

GESTAPO	Geheime Staats Polizei, Secret Service
HJ	Hitler Jugend, Hitler Youth
NAZI	Nationalsozialismus National Socialism
NSDAP	Nationalsozialistische Deutsche Arbeiterpartei, National Socialist German Workers' Party
SA	Sturmabteilung, Brown Shirts
SS	Schutzstaffel, Black Shirts

ABOUT THE AUTHOR

A native of Berlin, Christiane Brandt Faris came to the United States in 1968. She has advanced degrees in German and English from Göttingen University and Bucknell and is a recipient of the German Cross of Merit. She is an emeritus professor of German and former chair of the Modern Languages Department at Oklahoma City University.

Christiane Brandt Faris is the author of *Juxtapositions: Brunel Faris and the Visual Arts in Oklahoma.*

CPSIA information can be obtained at www.ICGtesting.com
Printed in the USA
BVOW01s1718081114

374214BV00002B/37/P